Pets *in* **Portraits**

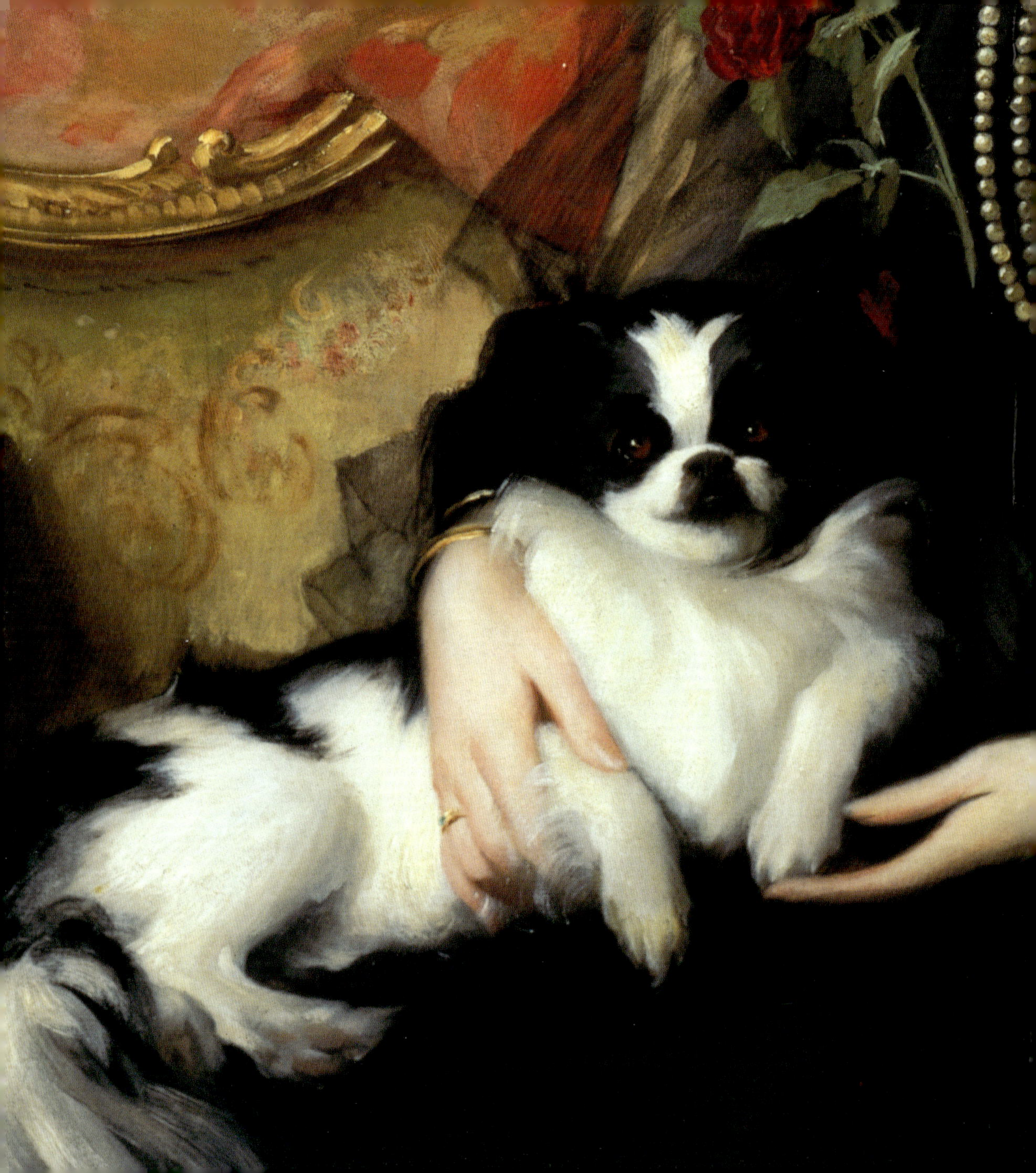

ROBIN GIBSON

with an introduction by

CHRIS PACKHAM

Pets *in* Portraits

NATIONAL PORTRAIT GALLERY, LONDON

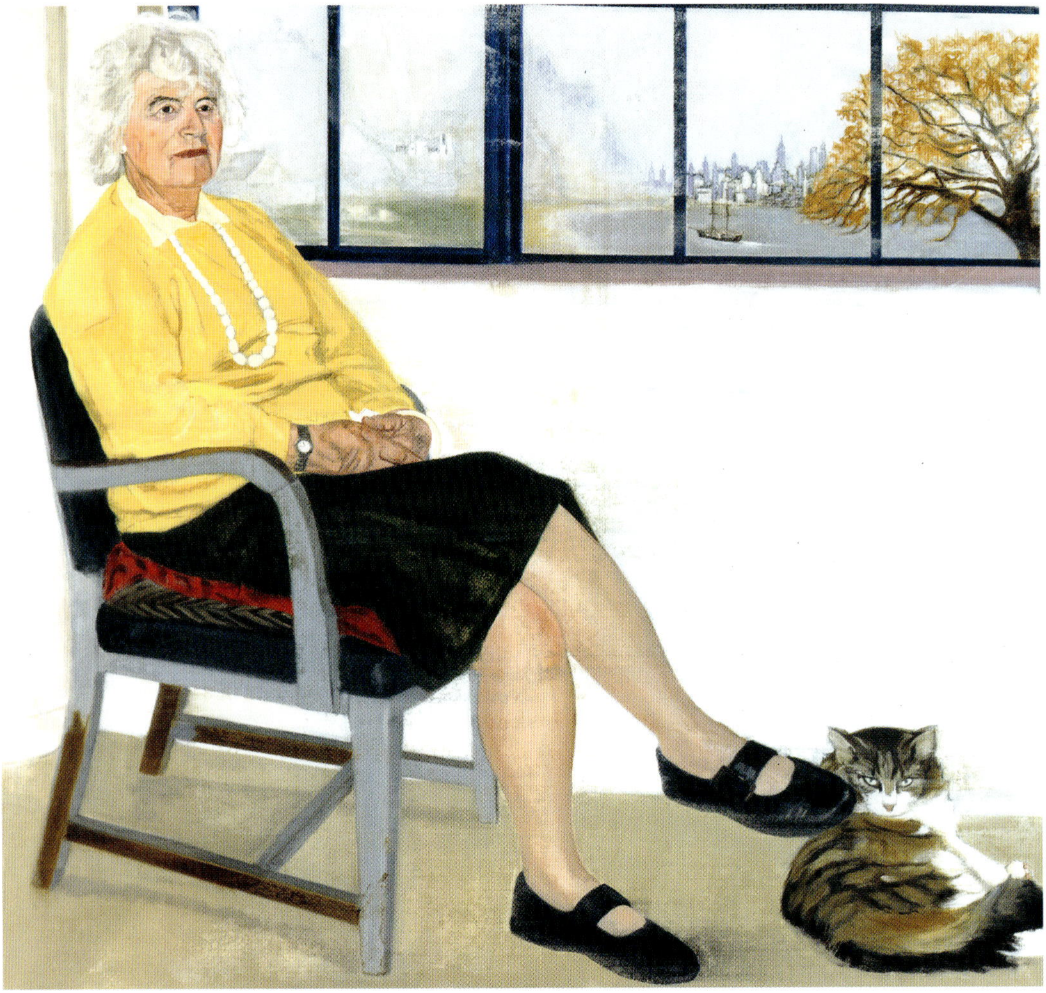

Jan Morris (b.1926) by Arturo Di Stefano, 2004–5. Oil on canvas, 1168 x 1219mm. NPG 6722. For her portrait, commissioned by the National Portrait Gallery, the travel writer Jan Morris requested 'an allegorical landscape of the imagination', and the inclusion of her Norwegian cat, Ibsen, was non-negotiable. The landscape beyond the studio window includes references to Wales, Venice, Trieste, Manhattan and Everest – all significant places in Morris's personal history. She has described sitting for the portrait as 'life enhancing' and 'one of the happiest experiences of my life'.

Contents

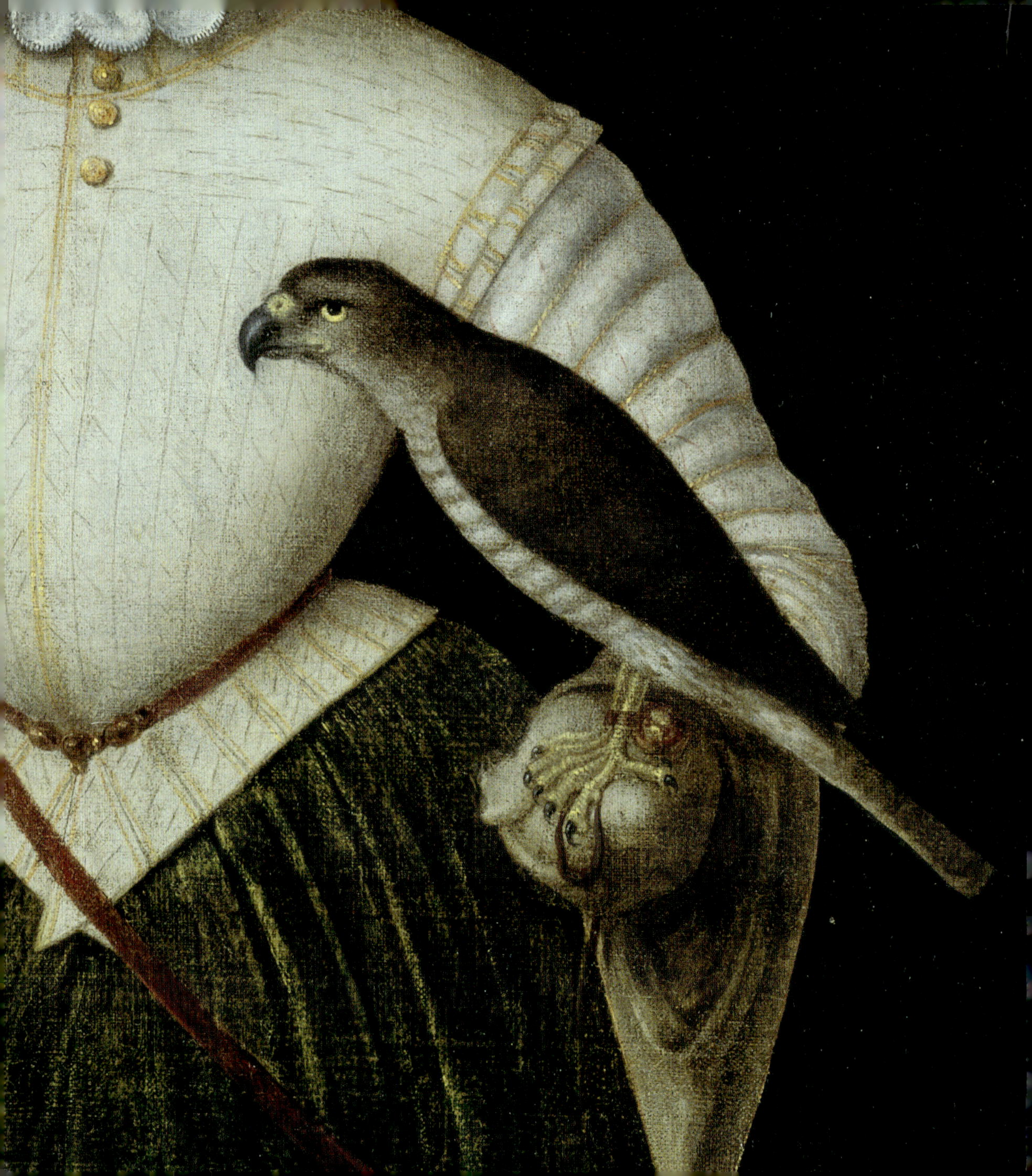

Introduction

CHRIS PACKHAM

I recall my first visit to the National Portrait Gallery with great clarity. While my father presided over a tour of the nation's castles and museums, my mother was in charge of art galleries, and my sister and I were enthusiastically led into the hallowed halls of the great and good in art. For her, the National Portrait Gallery was a favourite: she liked portraits; she easily enjoyed an instantaneous connection with other people, who, what or wherever they were. But as a child I didn't, couldn't read humans. I didn't really look at their faces, so being placed before a painting of one and asked to respond was difficult and disagreeable. I remember on that wet afternoon my poor mum's ebullience being dampened by my reluctance to do little but seek out animals in the portraits, peering into the dark corners of aged canvases in search of wild birds and mammals and even domestic pets. I imagined them as incidental or accidental inclusions; I wondered why there were so few, why so many were dead and why the humans seemed to be paying them so little attention. After all, these creatures were the stars, the far more beautiful and important things!

Detail from King James I of England and VI of Scotland (1566–1625) by an unknown artist, late sixteenth century (see page 8). NPG 63

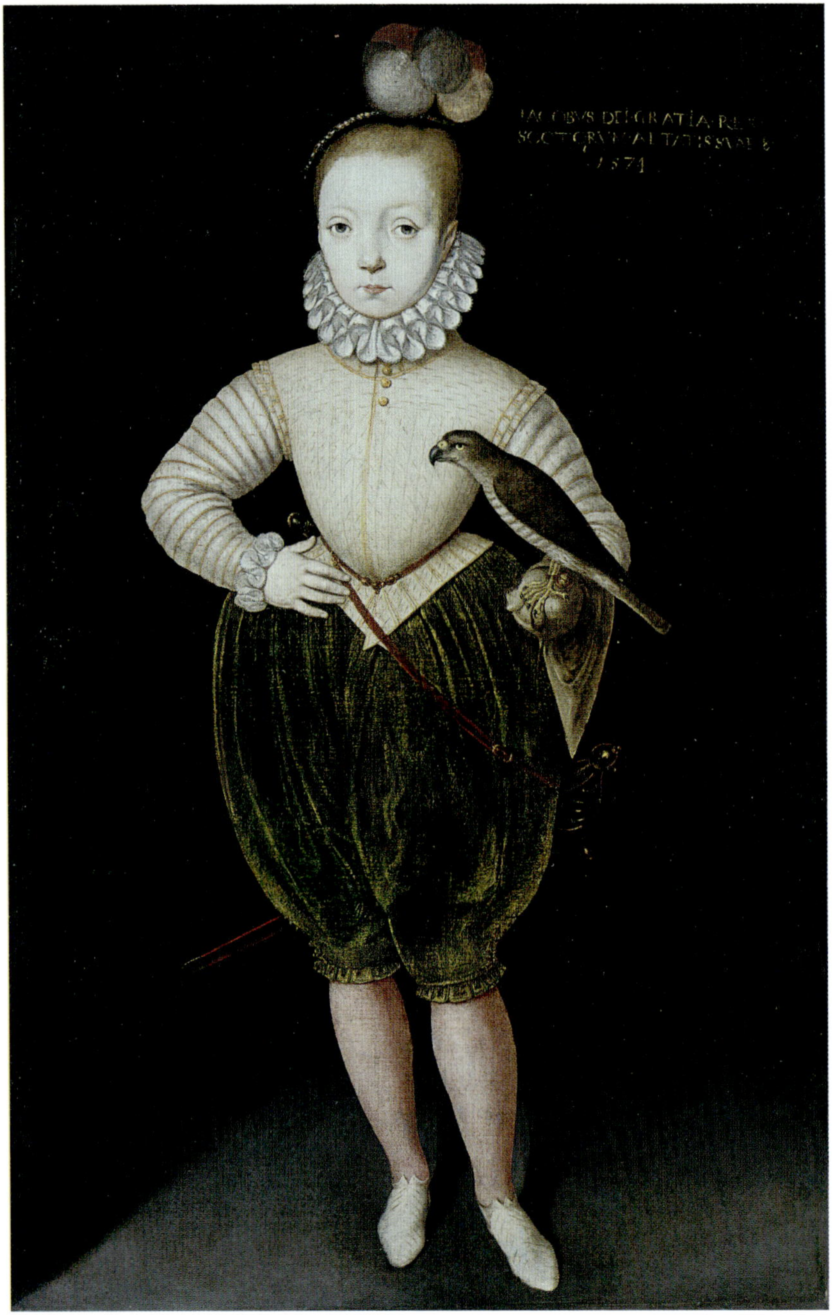

King James I of England and
VI of Scotland (1566–1625) by an
unknown artist, late sixteenth century.
Oil on canvas, 1181 x 730mm. NPG 63

Thus it's a pleasure to return to the Gallery as an adult who has subsequently studied our own species with a keen naturalist's eye, from which no detail escapes scrutiny, to provide a more balanced appraisal of some of those portraits that feature other animals, and maybe throw some small light on them, their characters, moods and very real personalities. Let's begin with the late-sixteenth-century painting (opposite) of King James I of England and his charming little raptor.

The bird is taut; it's drawn, primed and tense. It is not just wary or curious, it's stressed, frightened and it's about to leap from its perch in a manic flurry of wings. But then this species, the sparrowhawk, is renowned for being highly strung – neurotic, even – a real challenge for any falconer. I can tell these things not from the shape and attitude of the hawk, but because, like the boy–king, I too have stood with one sat on my fist. I have worried and fretted over the mood of my fragile companion, whose state of mind constantly troubled mine. But the choice of bird in this portrait is in itself vexing, as its inclusion is no accident. In portraits from this age the presence of animals is normally a critically considered part of the composition, often intended to reflect status. So why is the young dandy posing with a bird that was normally the charge of the priest?

The art and practice of falconry was bedevilled with formal codes, and one from *The Boke of Saint Albans*, which dates from 1486, prescribed the species that any man could keep, fly and hunt with. As a king, which he had been from the age of one, James should be standing with the world's largest falcon, the gyrfalcon, a powerful, muscular and extraordinarily beautiful bird from Iceland or Greenland. But maybe this scholarly and intellectual monarch, who went on to reign over England, Scotland and Ireland for twenty-two years, refused to be intimidated by such protocols. Maybe he enjoyed the challenge of taming one of nature's most notorious firebrands, just as I did. Perhaps this dowdy hawk was his favourite and, like me, he had taken some pleasure in its successful training. But, then, it is about to upset his fey pose, ruffle his ruff – and leave a deposit on his dainty slippers. That's birds for you.

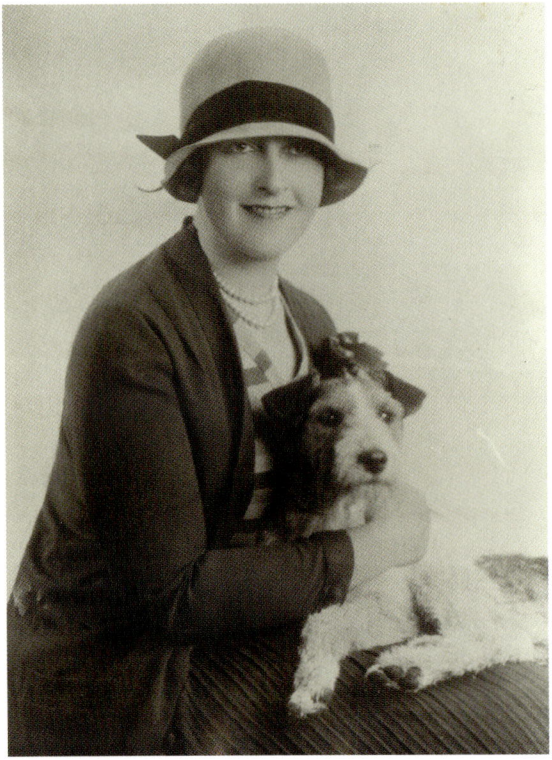

Agatha Christie (1890–1976)
by unidentified Free Press
photographer, 1920s.
Vintage print, 167 x 114mm.
NPG x135637

Birds are every bit as manipulative and challenging as a characterful dog, like the bright-eyed terrier with which Agatha Christie is wrestling in this lovely 1920s photograph (left). She is not only caressing the little terror, she is clearly restraining it, leaning forward to clutch it to her chest and preventing it from rushing towards whatever is dominating its attention. A sausage held by the photographer perhaps! And this no doubt recurrent challenge that I like to imagine is what has promoted her slightly desperate smile. But this trial also tells us that Christie very clearly wanted her canine companion in the picture. This is a photograph of the novelist and *her* dog, not of her and *a* dog. This is no surprise. She had loved dogs from an early age, kept them all her life and described very possibly the cheeky chap in this image, a wire-haired terrier called Peter, as 'a dog in a thousand'. She even dedicated one of her sixty-six novels to him. And it's this clear connection, her obvious affinity with her dog, that makes this portrait successful. It makes me smile, too; it makes me like her through simple association: that global and historical feeling of kinship for a species with whom we commonly form significant relationships.

Ponting's portrait of Robert Falcon Scott's accomplice Cecil Henry Meares and his dog Osman (right) tells a very different story. It's a joyless scene from the frozen south, and the man's frosted beard and clothing, his outstretched arm, betray a working dependency. On some polar expeditions the dogs pulled the men and their packs over miles of ice at horribly cold temperatures – but not Scott's. On his fateful trek he took ponies and motor sledges and not enough dogs, allegedly because he refused to countenance eating them as part of the process. Roald Amundsen, the Norwegian with whom Scott competed in the race to the South Pole, was more pragmatic – and succeeded, and survived. Osman got back and lived out his life in New Zealand. Meares and Ponting also lived. And of the portrait? Well, most of

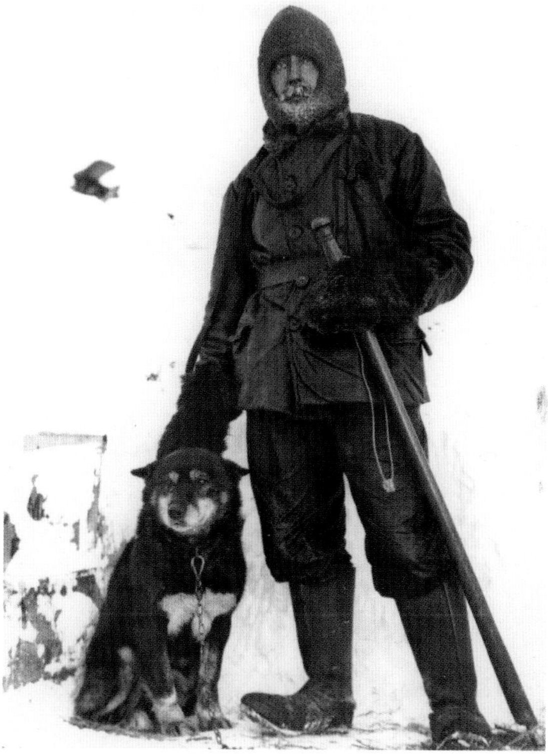

Cecil Henry Meares (1877–1937) by Herbert George Ponting, 1911. Bromide print, 454 x 330mm. NPG P209

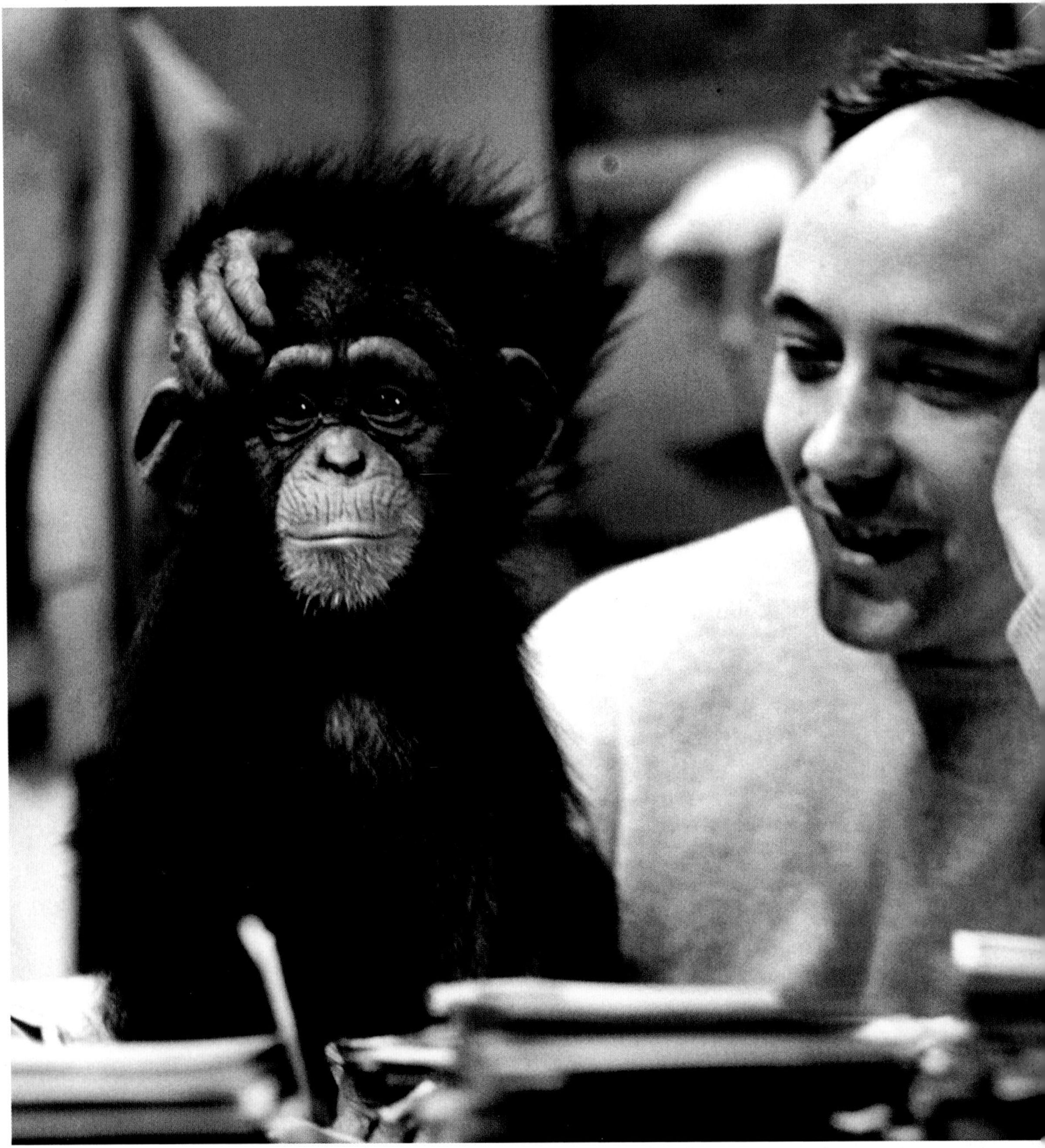

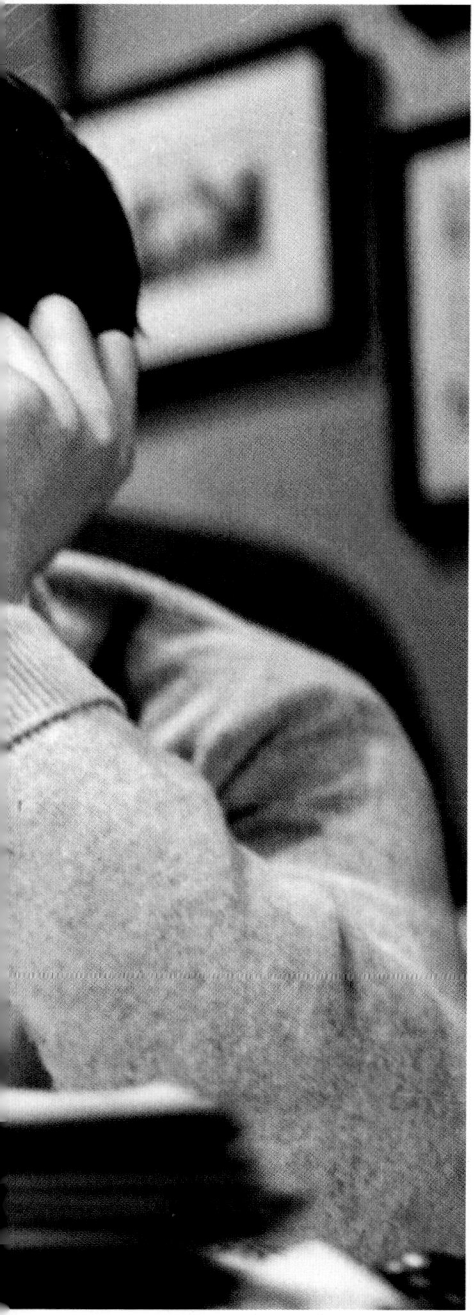

us can't even imagine the conditions. I hope the pair found some comfort in each other's company.

At some time in the 1950s someone gave Congo, the chimpanzee in this photograph (opposite), a pencil that it used to 'draw'. It later went on to become a renowned 'artist' – and not only among zoologist and broadcaster Desmond Morris's set of animal behaviourists. Picasso also owned one of Congo's 'pieces', Miró swapped two of his for one of the ape's, and, needless to say, Dalí made a vainglorious statement comparing Congo to Jackson Pollock. In 1957 the Institute of Contemporary Arts mounted a Congo exhibition, and in 2005 Bonhams auction house sold three of his 'pieces' for £14,400. Morris maintains that the star of TV's *Zoo Time* had a basic understanding of composition, and that its own favourite was a radiating fan pattern. Congo died of TB in 1965, aged ten. In Herbert K. Nolan's photograph the infant ape is frustrated while Morris is elated, revelling in the relationship he has forged with him. Cover the left half of the photo with your hand hiding Congo, show it to someone and ask them what Morris is looking at. I'll bet you a pound they will say a child, a baby. Morris is smitten, enraptured but perhaps spilling a little smug admiration, like a deluded parent inflating the accomplishments

Desmond Morris (b.1928) with Congo by Herbert K. Nolan, July 1956. Bromide print, 228 x 292mm. NPG x24198

of their child. Or maybe that's just my cynicism, motivated by the benefit of contemporary analysis of the lack of scientific rigour employed in those very early days of simian research. Maybe it's envy, as such contact is now forbidden due to that same scientific rigour. It's a marvellous picture that perfectly illustrates the very close relationship between us and the hairy apes.

Lastly, and forgive my indulgence, here (opposite) is a photograph of me with Itchy and Scratchy, my beloved miniature poodles. I include it to bring this entertaining and interesting collection of animal portraits completely up to date. It's a 'selfie', a digital self-portrait taken on a smartphone, of the type typically posted on social media. More than 880 billion photographs will be taken this year, and the single most popular genre is the 'selfie'. They have a poor reputation, seen as narcissistic, a fad for teenagers or to reinforce sexual stereotyping, but many, like this one, are made for private use, shared between friends by text or email. The obviously restrictive nature of the camera and the technique means they are snapshots, moments, rarely pictorially considered and thus short on artistic ambition. But they are 'of the age', and, given that prime ministers and presidents as well as passing pop stars are making them, I feel sure that some will one day find their way into gallery collections for the same simple reason that all the portraits in this book and in the National Portrait Gallery are displayed – they communicate instantly, easily and effectively, whether intra- or inter-specifically.

Chris Packham,
New Forest, Hampshire, July 2014

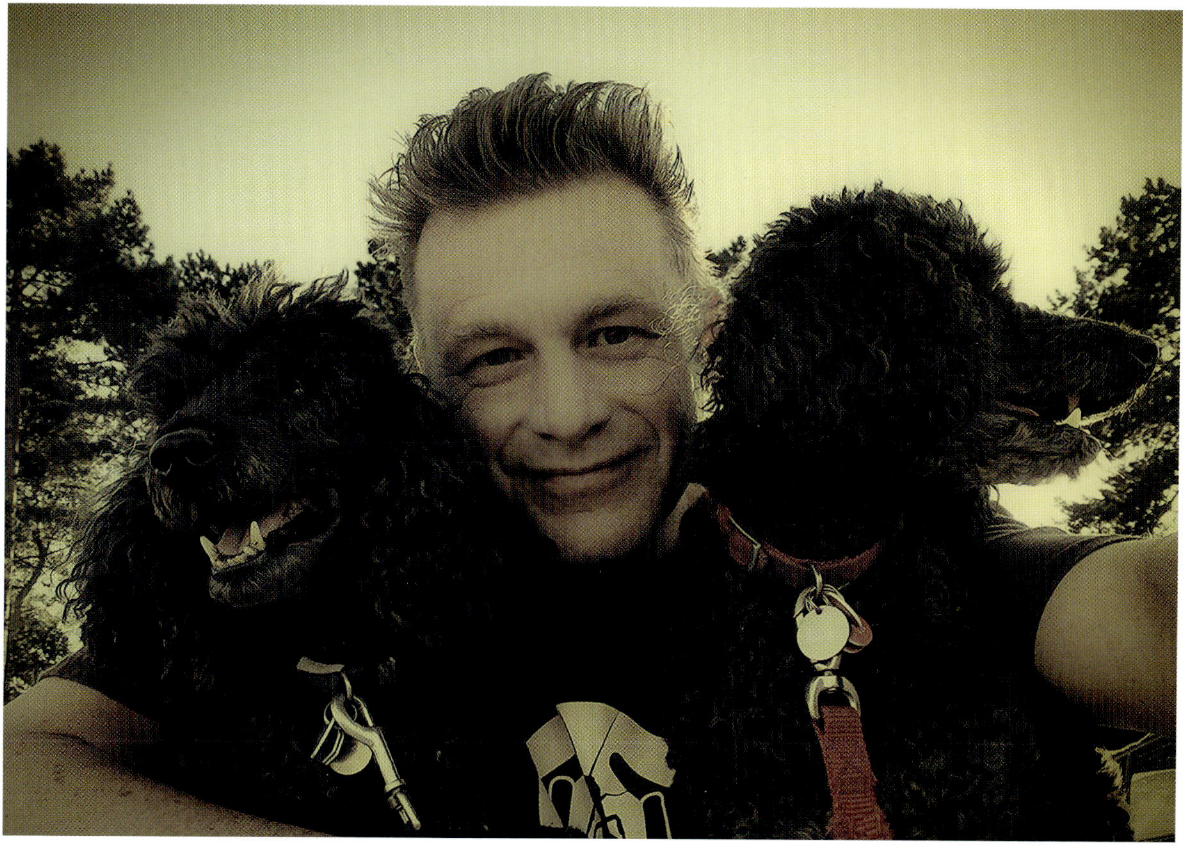

Chris Packham (b.1961) with Itchy and Scratchy, self-portrait, 2014. Digital photograph

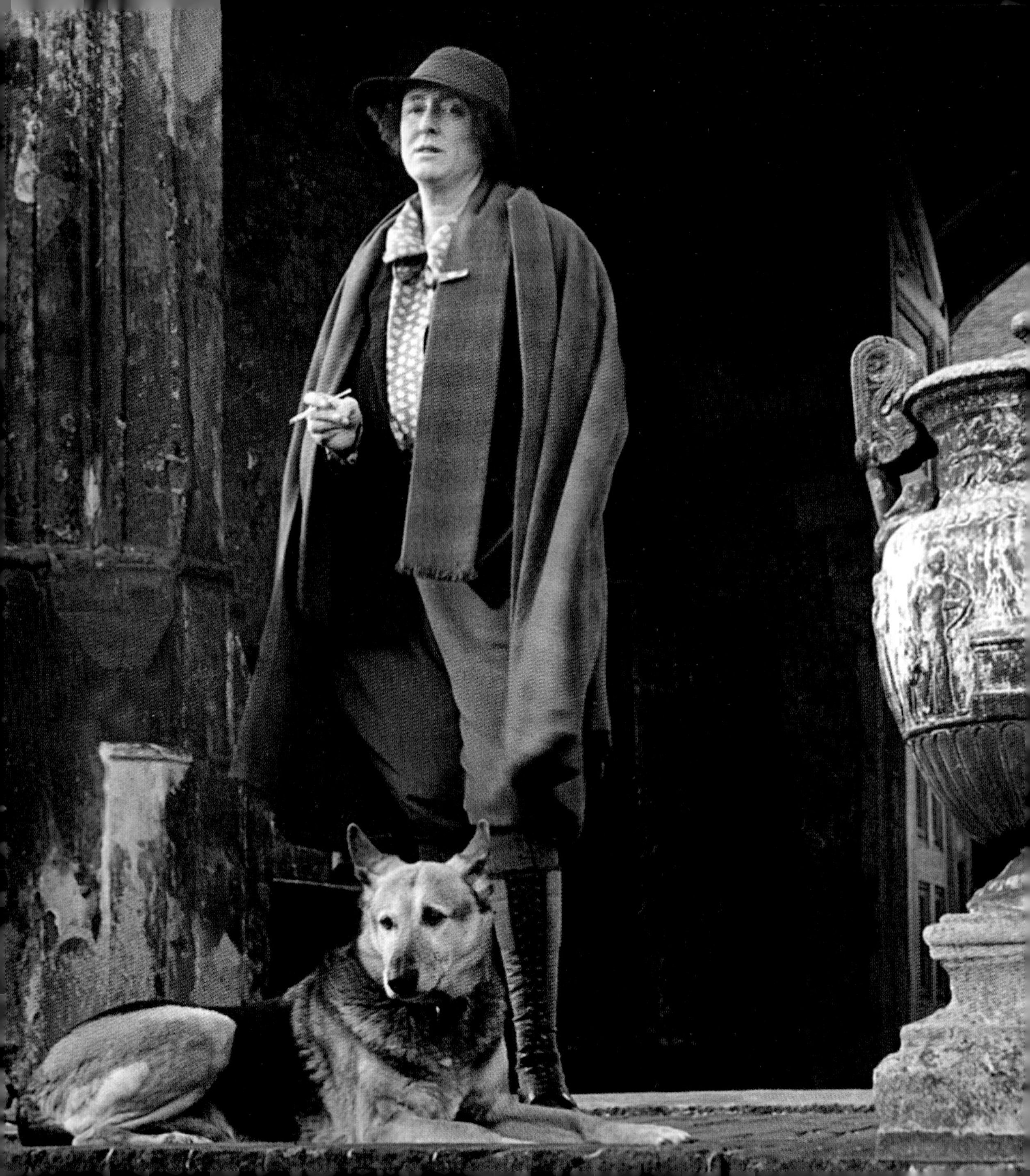

The Face in the Corner

This book is about the various animals that appear in portraits in the National Portrait Gallery, but it is also about the owners of the animals who commissioned the portraits. If we take the presence of horses in portraits for granted as the one universal means of transportation until the early twentieth century, there are many other reasons why someone should wish to have a particular animal included. In a sixteenth- or seventeenth-century painting, the animal almost certainly carried some symbolic significance and formed part of the artist's commentary on his subject. Later, in portraits of the landed gentry, an animal might serve as an indication of a lifestyle and status or, in a similar way, be little more than a fashion accessory in a portrait of a lady. Partly thanks to better documentation, it is not until well into the eighteenth century that we can determine whether the animal is a treasured pet and companion rather than simply part of the general *mise-en-scène*. Whatever the reason for inclusion, we may be sure that the animal's significance is in some way personal to the message that the artist and his sitter wished to convey to the viewer. Thus in

Detail from Vita Sackville-West and Martha by John Gay, 1948 (see page 117). NPG x47302

portraits that, like many of those in the National Portrait Gallery, were created for public and official purposes, animals tend to appear far less frequently.

Portraiture is possibly the most accessible branch of the visual arts, and the spectator can relate directly to and form opinions on the appearance, character and status of the subject perhaps more quickly than with any other form of painting or sculpture. For that reason it is easy to take the presence of animals, even if not always confined to the corner of the pictures, for granted, and few commentators on portraiture have devoted any attention to them. 'People and their pets'-type pictures, where the animal participates in the portrait on more or less equal terms with its human companion, are a comparatively recent phenomenon and coincide with a general shift towards greater informality in portraiture. The trend was perhaps begun by the gifted Victorian animal painter Sir Edwin Landseer, but only fully comes into its own with the rise of photojournalism, as the illustrations in this book demonstrate. With very few exceptions, modern painting has taken little interest in animals, and the concurrent and gradual decline of portraiture as a major art form seems to reflect this.

Dogs in particular have been the companions of man since pre-civilisation, and their inclusion in a portrait may seem, in a sense, no more remarkable than the usual essential ingredients of clothes or furniture. The ownership of land since time immemorial has entailed not only money and power, and the country houses and portraits with which to commemorate it, but also hunting and shooting and the dogs and hounds that were a necessary part of this privileged activity. In medieval times, hunting, usually with elegant and aristocratic greyhounds, had been an essential ingredient of the courtly tapestries and manuscript illuminations of the period. In the Netherlands in the seventeenth century and in eighteenth-century Britain in particular, schools of painting developed that were devoted solely to the genre of hunting in one form or another. We should now think it strange indeed to visit a great country house and not find successive portraits of the head of the family with his dogs or horses, or with his friends and retainers out fox hunting or returning from a day's shoot.

Portraiture, however, is not all social history, and in the fifteenth century it was as a cultural phenomenon, one manifestation of the visual arts and of easel painting in particular, that it began to appear as a genre in its own right. For Flemish artists, it was only one step from the inclusion in an altarpiece of a portrait of the donor, the man who had paid for the picture, to painting a separate picture of the man in his own right. Animals also first made their appearance in Gothic and early Renaissance religious paintings, but usually with a symbolic significance that would perhaps inevitably be carried over into portraiture for several hundred years. Dogs had been largely ignored by the Bible, except as scavengers, but they (and horses) were characterised by the Roman author Pliny the Elder as the most faithful friends of man. It was this classical and increasingly pantheistic view that held sway in the late Middle Ages, and fidelity remained the primary significance of the dog's appearance in early religious painting and portraiture. Its meaning could be further refined, so that a white greyhound, so often seen with the three kings in paintings of the Adoration of the Magi, is not only an emblem of fidelity to the new-born Saviour but, with its courtly associations, is also a sign of the visitors' high birth, and its whiteness a symbol of purity and blessedness. Dogs were also the emblems of St Eustace and St Hubert, patron saints of hunting and, by an elaborate pun, of one of the most powerful religious orders, the Dominicans (*Domini canes* – the dogs of the Lord). Cats fared badly. They were seen as creatures of the night and thus associated with the devil, witches and lechery, or at best with sloth, since they were inclined to sleep during the day. For that reason, and though they appear in seventeenth-century Dutch genre paintings, they were scarcely ever seen in religious works or (with one notable exception) in portraiture until the eighteenth century.

Birds, however, are frequently found in early Renaissance paintings, and, although never a common feature of portraiture, their presence there is often a survival of their early emblematic significance. The goldfinch, well known in representations of the Madonna and Child, was emblematic of the Passion of Christ because it lived and fed on thistles, which were equated with the crown of thorns. Its bright plumage in any case made it a popular pet, and it is sometimes seen in portraits of children, a general symbol of innocence. In later seventeenth- and eighteenth-century portraits it is just as likely to be any wild bird, often seen rather cruelly tied to a string, and really of no greater significance than any other wild creature kept as a pet. Parrots, including cockatoos and parakeets, however, were expensive imports; they were meant to be noticed and since the fifteenth century had acquired a double meaning. In that they could imitate their masters' voice, their significance was similar to that of the faithful dog: indeed their inclusion in paintings of the Madonna was said to be because they could say 'Ave'. A green parrot, in a somewhat convoluted simile that survived into seventeenth-century emblem books, was also a symbol of virginity because the green of its plumage never became wet when it rained, unlike the green foliage and grass of mother earth. As such, a green parakeet is seen perching on another later symbol of virginity, an orange tree, in the portrait by Nicolas de Largillière of the children of James II (fig. 1).

The lamb or sheep carries a similarly elaborate significance as far as portraits are concerned. An established Christian symbol for Christ, it was also the emblem of St Agnes and in a portrait can occasionally be linked with her name or her virtues. In seventeenth-century emblem books, however, its interpretation is specifically classical and refers to Aries, the appropriate sign of the zodiac. Aries is the constellation of spring time, and a ram or sheep shown in a portrait being garlanded with flowers by a Restoration beauty such as Nell Gwyn (fig. 2) is a sign that we are required to view the lady in the guise of Primavera, the embodiment of youth and fecundity. By the eighteenth century the sheep's significance has declined to the purely pastoral, and it is a common feature in rococo portraits of ladies as Arcadian shepherdesses or may even appear simply as a cuddly pet in some portraits of children.

Fig. 1. Detail from the portrait of Prince James Francis Edward Stuart and his sister, Louisa Maria Theresa, by Nicolas de Largillière, 1695 (see page 58). NPG 976

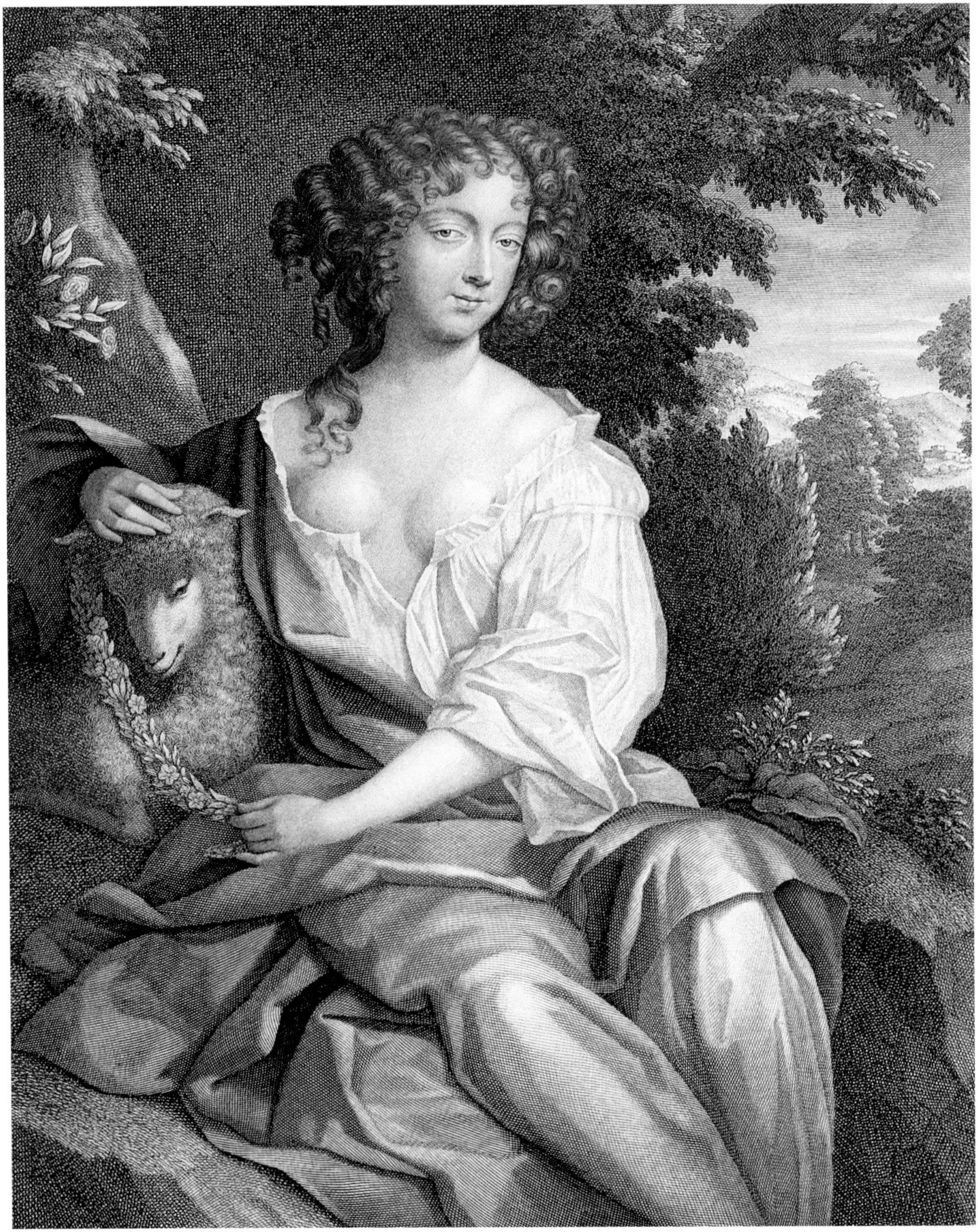

The first notable animal in European portraiture is without doubt the little lap dog in the foreground of the famous Arnolfini wedding portrait in the National Gallery by the Flemish artist Jan van Eyck. Painted in 1434, the dog is of course, like almost everything else in the painting, a symbol, but, again like everything else in this most perfect example of early Renaissance humanism, also a totally natural and believable presence. Influences spread slowly, and it was not until a hundred years later that the great Italian painter Titian would begin to include dogs in many of his portraits – from the magnificent racing dog of the Emperor Charles V to the little toy spaniel curled up on the table next to the Duchess Eleanora Gonzaga. Indeed, British painting was still at this time in its infancy, and not until Sir Anthony van Dyck arrived here, nearly two hundred years after the painting of the Arnolfini portrait, would a dog in a British portrait achieve anything more than heraldic significance.

This lamentable fact is purely a reflection of the off-shore status of British painting and in no way of the status of the British pet. Sixteenth-century Britain is as fertile a source of famous dog stories as any century since. Payments for Henry VIII's spaniel Cutte were recorded in the royal accounts, and across the border Mary Queen of Scots was an even more celebrated dog-owner. While she was Queen, two loaves a day and 'blue velvet collars for the Queen's little dogs' had been provided. In captivity, she wrote to the Archbishop of Glasgow asking about a couple of 'pretty little dogs' from Lyons: 'my only

Fig. 2. Line engraving after a portrait of Eleanor 'Nell' Gwyn as 'Spring' with a sheep, by Gerard Valck, after Sir Peter Lely, c.1670. 349 x 254mm. NPG 3811

pleasure is in all the little animals I can get. They must be sent in baskets, well stored so as to keep them warm.' It was one of these little dogs that accompanied her, concealed under her skirt, to her execution. Spotted with her blood, the faithful beast was discovered between her severed head and trunk, and could only forcibly be separated from her corpse. More famous by name was Sir John Harington's dog Bungey, who on several occasions carried letters from his house near Bath to the court at Greenwich and back again. Bungey also transported two flagons of sherry across country, hiding one when he found it too heavy and returning for it later; more practically, he found Sir John's purse full of gold when he had lost it. Harington was so proud of Bungey that he had his picture engraved as frontispiece to his translation of Ludovico Ariosto's *Orlando Furioso* in 1591 and later wrote Bungey's biography and sent it to another dog-lover, Henry, Prince of Wales.

These stories can only have served to reinforce the dog's significance as a symbol of fidelity, but none appears in their masters' portraits. One of the few exceptions to the general rule about the lack of animals in early British portraiture is an engaging small panel of Mary Stuart's hated persecutor, Elizabeth I (fig. 3), which shows an adoring small, white lap dog of the same bichon type that Mary would have owned, which had also appeared in the Arnolfini portrait. Mention must also be made of the great exception to the rule about cats: the remarkable portrait of Henry, 3rd Earl of Southampton, by John de Critz, painted in 1603 (fig. 4). It commemorates Southampton's imprisonment in the Tower, and whether the cat was a real one or not, its function in the picture is to underline

Fig. 3. Elizabeth I by Marcus Gheeraerts the Elder, c.1580–85. Oil on panel, 457 x 381mm. © Private collection

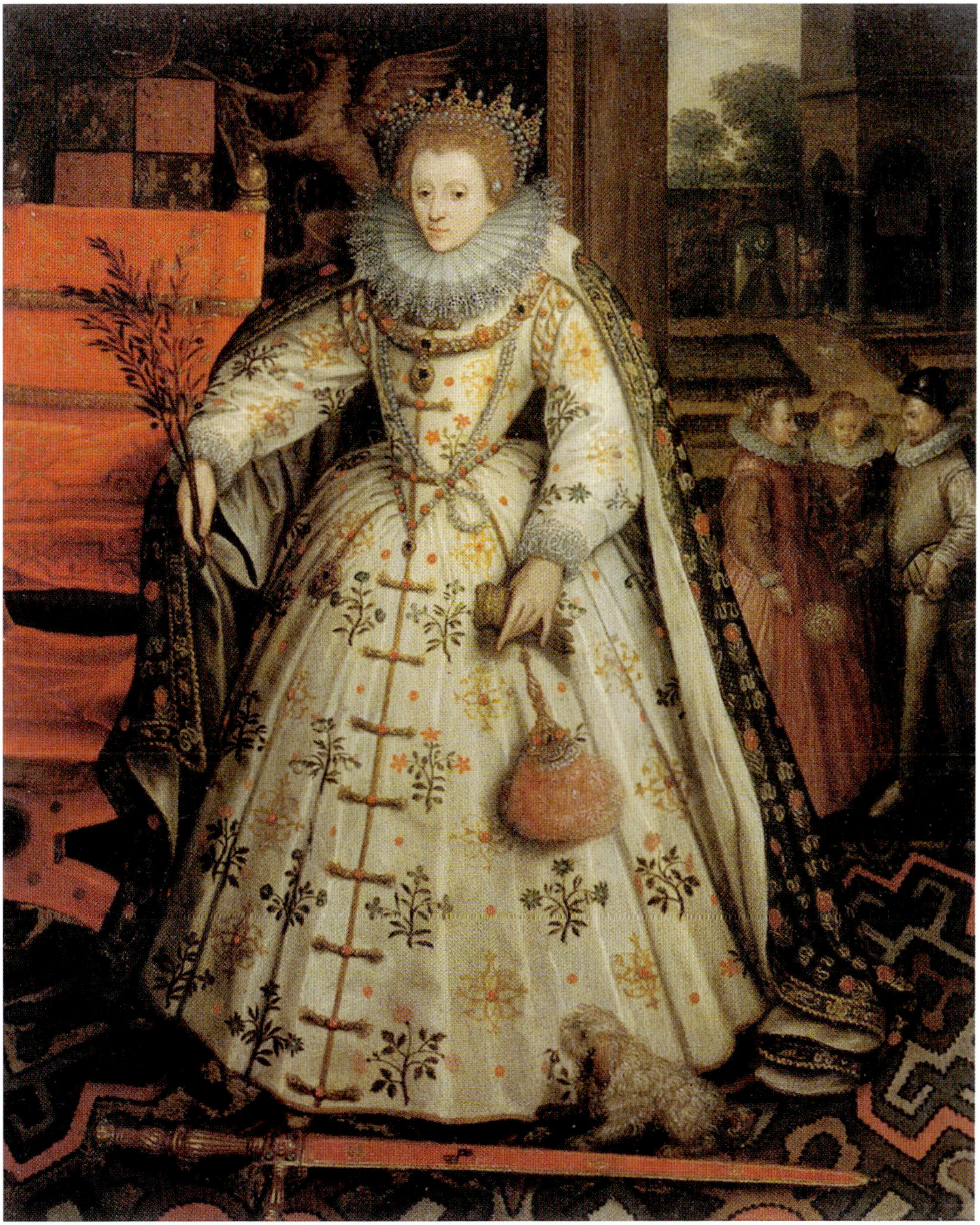

the prisoner's solitude, the cat being his only companion during his captivity. While there may in its presence be a trace of the cat's old associations with witchery and bad luck, it demonstrates nevertheless a rather modern and more psychological use of animal symbolism, more commonly found in much later portraits. In the late Victorian portrait of Charles Reade, for instance (see page 93), the companionship of the dog and the cats helps to emphasise the essential isolation necessary to the creative writer, as it does in much the same way for the enforced loneliness of the sick in Sir Francis Chantrey's amusing self-portrait drawing (page 81).

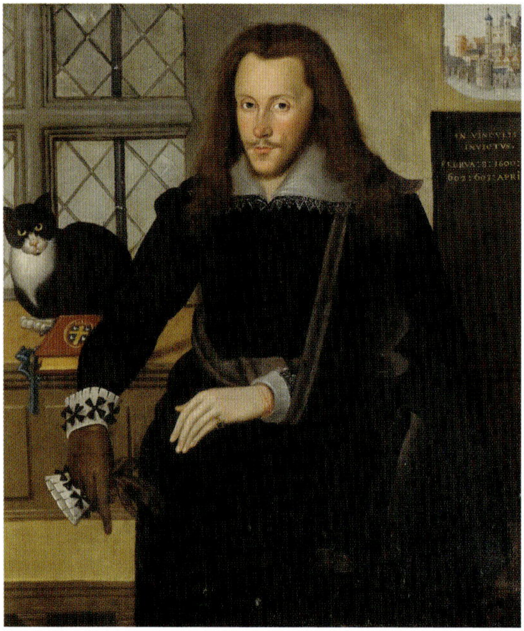

Fig. 4. Henry Wriothesley, 3rd Earl of Southampton, by John de Critz, 1603. Oil on canvas, 1092 x 876mm. Private collection

With the presence in the 1630s of Sir Anthony van Dyck at the court of Charles I, dogs (though not cats) in portraits become a commonplace. The trigger for this may to an extent have been Van Dyck's study of the works of Titian, most noticeable in his full-length portraits of men of power and influence, such as the Duke of Richmond with his huge greyhound in the Metropolitan Museum, New York. There seems little doubt, however, that Charles's French queen, Henrietta Maria, also played a significant role, and the toy spaniels, which were almost certainly her introduction to the court, can be seen romping around in all Van Dyck's paintings of the Royal Family and children. Paradoxically, these toy spaniels, which came to be known as King Charles's and can be found in so many paintings of Charles I's family, are not found in any painting of his son Charles II, after whom they were named, with the solitary exception of the one reproduced here, made when he was a baby (fig. 5).

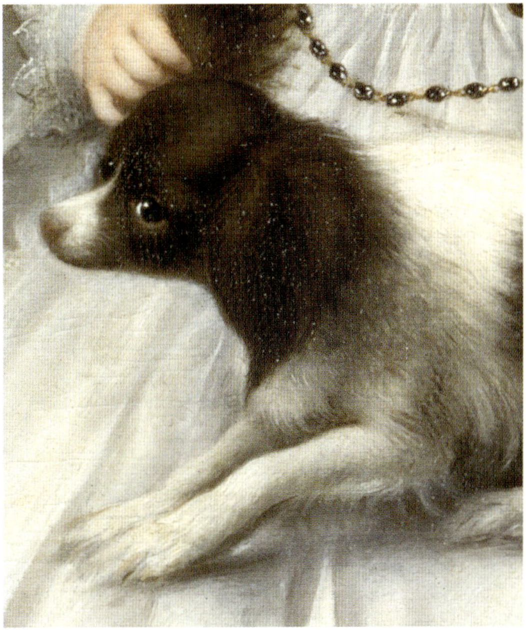

Fig. 5. Detail from Charles II as a baby by an unknown artist, 1630 (see page 49). NPG 6403

Despite the spaniels' by now rather superficial symbolism as emblems of fidelity, their appearance in Van Dyck's paintings introduces another strand to the saga of animals in portraiture, that of the fashion accessory. Fashions for certain breeds of dog are a well-known phenomenon and, with their royal associations, toy spaniels have remained popular domestic pets and have been one of the most enduring breeds to figure in both British and foreign portraiture, especially with women and children. They may be found again and again in portraits throughout the seventeenth and eighteenth centuries, and they make a determined revival in the nineteenth, when the young Queen Victoria had her spaniel Dash painted by Landseer. Their only serious rival in the seventeenth century for inclusion in portraits of women seems to have been the small Italian greyhound (page 57), an even more delicate import than the toy spaniel, but one that lent an elegant and slightly more sporty air to the sitter, especially appropriate for classically orientated baroque symbolism such as that of the goddess of hunting, Diana.

The standard symbolism in baroque portraiture of the dog's fidelity to its master continues the basically Christian visual metaphor of medieval times, and it is significant that its last (and most magnificent) gasp in the National Portrait Gallery's collection is to be found in the 1695 portrait by a Catholic painter, de Largillière, of the Catholic children of James II, the 'Old Pretender' and his sister (page 58). As usual in such dynastic portraits, the boy (and heir) is given a hunting dog of some splendour for his companion while the little girl, like the daughter in the Vyner family (page 54), has to make do with some emblematic flowers as more suited to her sex and status. In this instance, the message could not be more clear: the exiled prince is seeking the fidelity of his subjects over the English Channel; his sister, holding a sprig of orange blossom, is a virgin and is (or will soon be) looking for a suitable husband. The splendid brass collar worn by the greyhound carries in this case no inscription, though in many such portraits it would have been inscribed with the name of its owner, thus proclaiming not only the identity of the portrait for all to see but also the sitter's wealth and dominion over those claiming loyalty to him.

There is of course no evidence whatsoever that the dogs shown in the de Largillière portrait belonged to the children, and many such emblematic pets, however realistically painted, were patently of the 'rent-a-dog' variety. Though the average princely or ducal kennels would have had no trouble in rustling up a suitable breed for a particular portrait, in many cases it seems probable that such animals no more belonged to the subject of the portrait than did the classical columns or orange trees in the picture. Indeed, in the hands of less skilled artists, animals are sometimes scarcely identifiable as anything other than dog- or horse-shaped accessories. This practice has of course never totally disappeared. In an amusing essay entitled 'Borrowed Dogs', the American photographer Richard Avedon, commenting on the artificiality of much photography of the previous generation, remembers with embarrassment how his parents would invariably beg the loan of a dog, sometimes from complete strangers, before taking a family photograph. They imagined, no doubt, like many before them, that the inclusion of an imposing beast would lend both the family and the photograph a certain dash and distinction.

The apparently heavy-handed, though to the contemporary viewer totally unremarkable, symbolism of the baroque was almost invariably practised in seventeenth-century Britain by painters from abroad and frequently from Catholic countries. In the eighteenth century, the Age of Reason, and in particular in Protestant liberty-conscious Britain, it could not survive, and the native painters of the first half of the century such as William Hogarth looked to the genre painting of seventeenth-century Protestant Holland for his inspiration. The conversation pieces of Hogarth and of his rivals such as Gawen Hamilton (pages 62–3) are full of dogs and cats included quite straightforwardly as part of the domestic scene. Cats indeed undergo a quite extraordinary U-turn in their fortunes. By the middle of the century, kittens, both cuddly and playful, are frequently seen in portraiture throughout Europe as suitable accessories for portraits of little girls, presumably under the assumption that that is what little girls are like – or, possibly, what they will grow up to be. Such unconscious sexual innuendo has been shown to play an increasing role in eighteenth- and early nineteenth-century portraiture, where the elements of a painting were no longer dictated by traditional conventions and symbols. In the case of the courtesan Kitty Fisher (page 73), however, the kitten seen fishing for golden opportunities is quite blatantly much more than a mere pun.

In an era of overriding humanism (and, it must also be admitted, of better documentation), pets in portraits were now, as often as not, not simply accessories but also specifically identifiable creatures with known names, lifespans and allegiances. The fact that many animals in portraits from the early eighteenth century onwards now become identifiable pets, is, of course, also partly due to the rise of a far more settled and affluent society, where working dogs and cats stood more chance of becoming household familiars or indeed prized sporting assets. To meet this development, there now began to appear in Britain a number of animal and sporting painters, including artists like Hogarth's near contemporary, John Wootton, and a little later the greatest of them all, George Stubbs. We know from a family group that Wootton owned his own Italian greyhound, but apart from painting the racehorses and hunts of his aristocratic patrons, he also painted their pet dogs. For Edward Harley, Earl of Oxford, he painted at least six portraits of the family's dogs, including the overweight and ageing spaniel Casey on a grandiose red cushion, and for the King's minister, Sir Robert Walpole, he did a mock-heroic portrait of his Italian hound, Patapan.

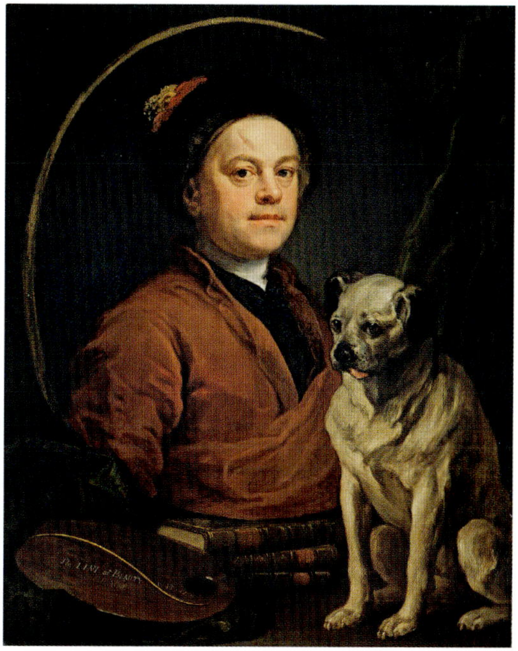

Fig. 6. *The Painter and His Pug* by William Hogarth, 1745. Oil on canvas, 900 x 699mm. Tate Gallery

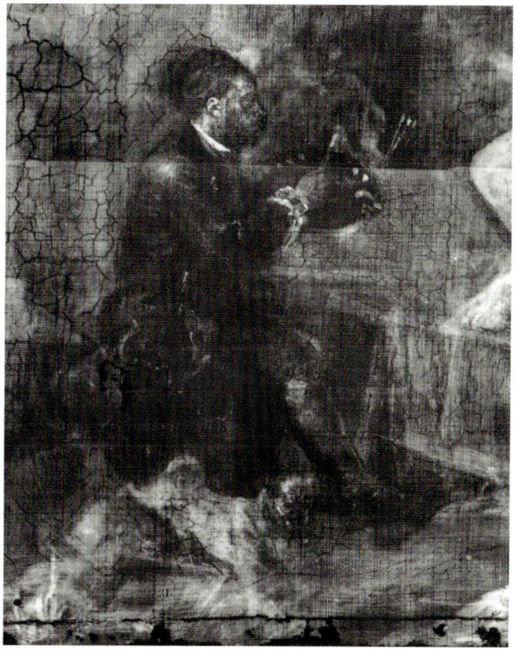

Fig. 7. X-ray of *Self-portrait Painting the Comic Muse* (detail) by William Hogarth, 1758. Oil on canvas, 451 x 425mm. NPG 289

It is against this background that the independent-minded Hogarth deployed his beloved pugs. The breed was originally introduced into Britain from Holland by William of Orange, and Hogarth is known to have possessed at least three pugs, of whom Trump, who figures so prominently in the famous self-portrait in the Tate Gallery, London (fig. 6), is the best known. Trump's presence reflects not only Hogarth's love and deep respect for the animal but, with his independent and no-nonsense outlook on life, is also a metaphor for the artist himself. As such, Trump appears on his own as the artist's commentator in several other

Hogarth paintings, for instance wearing a wig and mocking the pomposity of naval officers in the group portrait of *Captain Lord George Graham in His Cabin* (National Maritime Museum, London). What is probably a later pug makes a surprising hidden appearance in the National Portrait Gallery's *Self-portrait Painting the Comic Muse* (fig. 7). Visible only in X-ray – probably after Hogarth decided he might have overstepped the mark – the pug is seen urinating on the artist's behalf on a pile of old-master paintings: a succinct comment on those collectors who preferred second-rate foreign imports to contemporary works by British artists.

Trump becomes in a sense Hogarth's alter ego, though in a much more flamboyant manner than other artists' pets. Sir Alfred Munnings (page 119) used one of his dogs in a satirical painting two centuries later, but it is perhaps only Landseer in the nineteenth century and Maggi Hambling (page 132) in the present day who have to a similar extent used their own and other animals to reflect their innermost ideas and indeed their own personalities. The German-born and sober-minded Johann Zoffany clearly derived simple pleasure from including his own white German spitz, Poma, in some of his paintings (fig. 8), so that she becomes a sort of covert signature. It is not clear whether Thomas Gainsborough may also have included his own dogs in some of his work, though they appear in portraits of his own family and on their own in the enchanting portrait of the two little dogs, *Tristram and Fox*, in the Tate Gallery, London. Gainsborough's genius as a painter of dogs has seldom been noticed, but stylistically in this he lies somewhere between Stubbs and Landseer. He also painted

Fig. 8. Mary and John Wilkes by Johann Joseph Zoffany, exhibited 1782. Oil on canvas, 1264 x 1003mm. NPG 6133

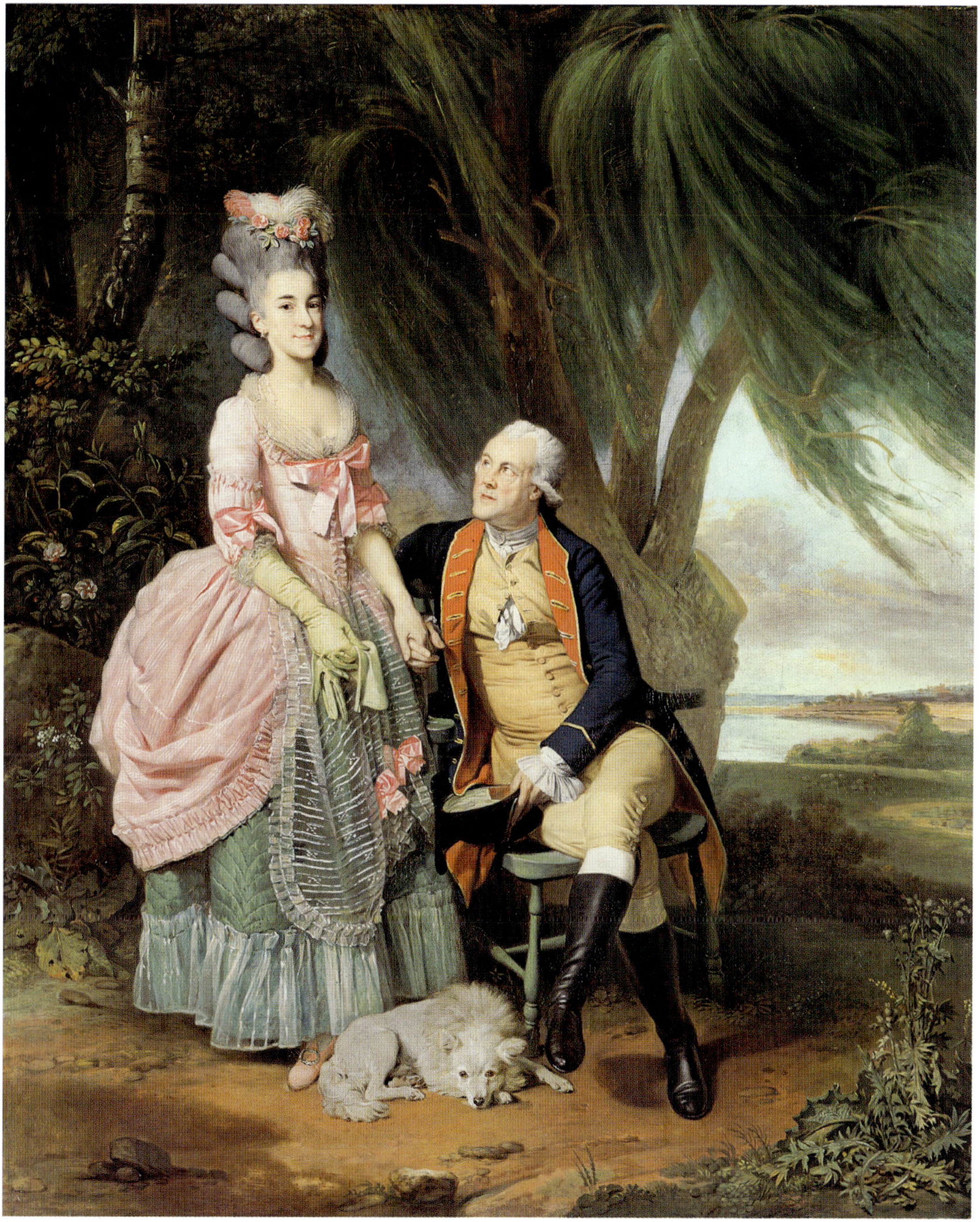

a portrait of his musician friend Carl Friedrich Abel's two white German spitzes, a breed that appears in the famous *The Morning Walk* in the National Gallery, London (fig. 9), and seems to have been one of the most fashionable dogs of the late 1770s and the 1780s. It seems quite likely that the paintings of Gainsborough and Zoffany, not to mention the influence of their expatriate German friends in the world of music and indeed of a German queen, Charlotte, were to a substantial extent jointly responsible for the popularity of the German spitz, often referred to at the time as a Pomeranian or fox dog. Fifty years later, the paintings of Landseer would do much the same for the increasing popularity of the Scottish deerhound and the Newfoundland.

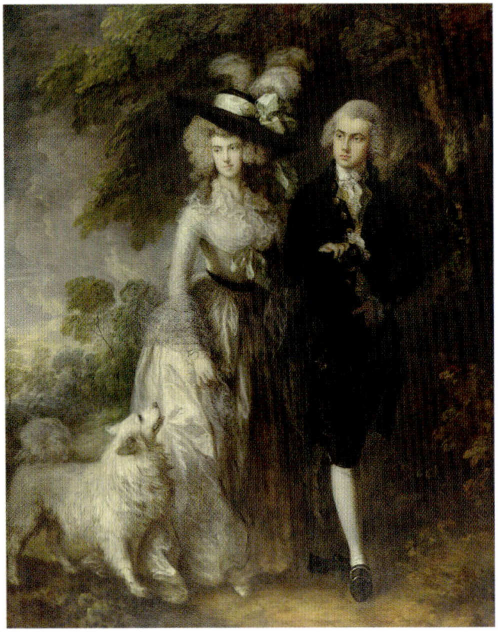

Fig. 9. Mr and Mrs William Hallett (*The Morning Walk*) by Thomas Gainsborough, 1785. Oil on canvas, 2360 x 1790mm. National Gallery

The association of the subject or indeed the artist of a portrait with an identifiable pet immediately adds a further dimension to our understanding of the characterisation. Admittedly, apart from proclaiming 'this is also a nice person who likes animals/hunting/shooting', it would probably in most cases only have been of significance to friends and family who knew the animal in question. It was clearly of importance to the sitter, however, and we find the poet William Shenstone (page 70) wondering whether his 'faithful Lucy' should be moved a bit to the left in order to improve the composition of his portrait, and the painter Angelica Kauffmann noting in her accounts, 'likewise the portrait of the pet dog' specifically mentioned for inclusion in her portrait of Thomas Jenkins and his niece (page 79). In the case of a subject like Sir Walter Scott, whose Scottish deerhound Maida had become nationally famous, not only from the reports of pilgrims to his house at Abbotsford but also through his writings, the artist Sir William Allan apparently felt that it would be unthinkable to exclude the dog, even though he had by all accounts died several years earlier (fig. 10).

The corollary to this is that the animal, as well as saying something about the subject, may also be representing someone absent from the portrait, and thereby conveying some sort of hidden message. How many people at the time would have known that Lady Caroline Lamb's little dog Phyllis and its jewelled bracelet (pages 84–5) were in fact gifts from a lover and therefore a semi-public admission, indeed a commemoration, of an illicit affair? In the portrait of Charles Reade (page 93), his mistress's dog Puff and her faintly sketched-in portrait on the wall stand in for Mrs Seymour, his lifelong companion, who probably for reasons of propriety could not herself be included in the portrait. The same is true to a slightly lesser extent of the photograph of Ellen Terry (page 101), since the dogs shown with her were an integral part of her relationship with Sir Henry Irving. Stretching the analogy further, we might speculate that the little dachshund Clytie, shown in Yousuf Karsh's photograph of Benjamin Britten (page 122) and bearing the name of Peter Pears's singing teacher, is also in a way a symbol of the composer's private life and of his relationship with Pears.

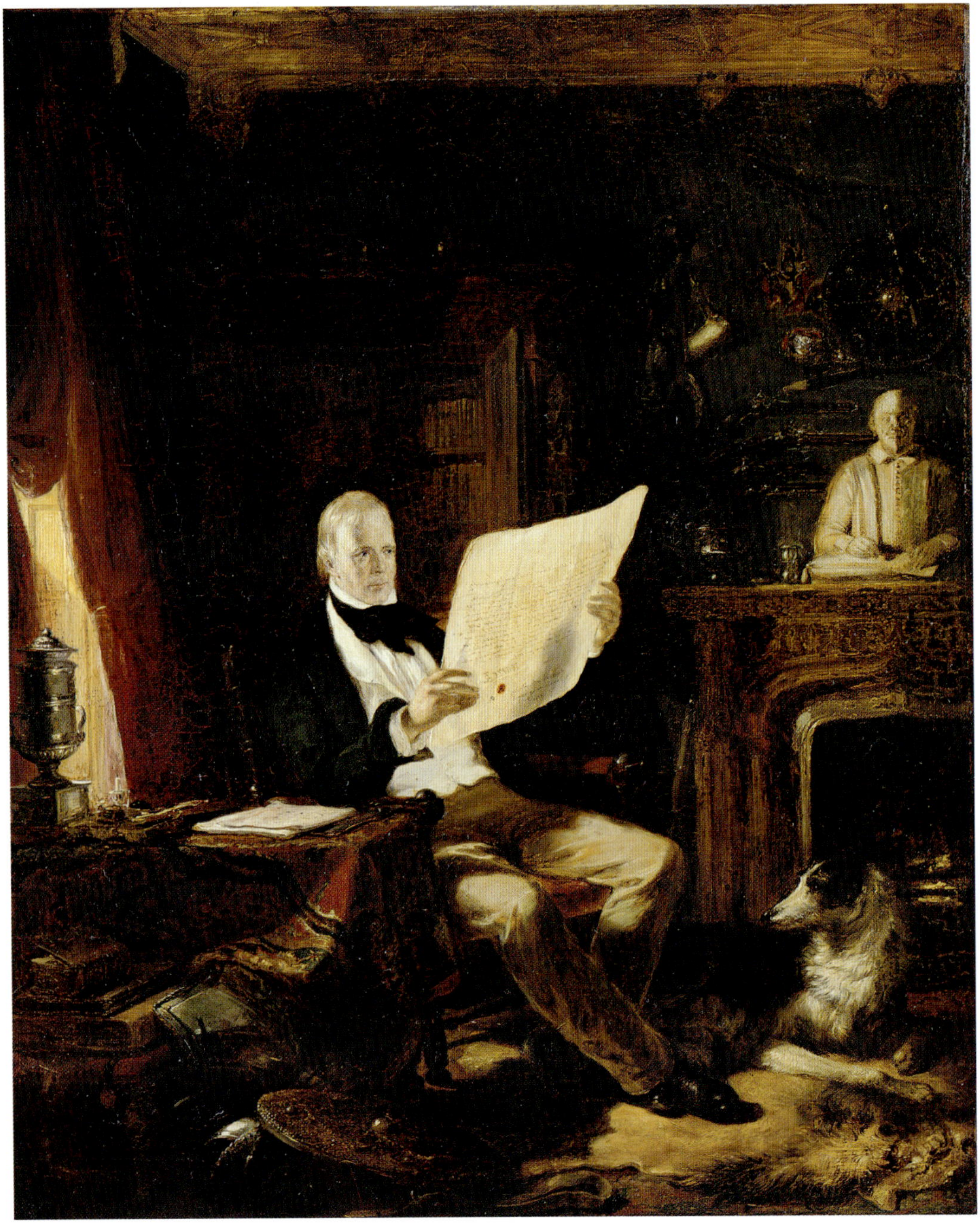

From absent lover to surrogate lover is only a short step, and a quick glance through the portraits in this book reveals how many distinguished pet owners were if not actually bachelors, at least widowed, divorced or past the passionate affairs of their youth. One such 'passionate' relationship one feels must probably have existed between the 'difficult' bachelor–poet William Shenstone and his 'faithful Lucy', and certainly between Edwin Landseer (pages 88–9), who never married, and some of his many dogs. The understanding and pathos with which Landseer was to imbue his portraits of dogs is unparalleled in art history, and Lassie and Rifa appear in his only self-portrait on intimate and equal footing with himself. For Elinor Glyn (page 112), now an ageing beauty settling down to an active retirement after a career littered with affairs, the two reliable cats came no doubt to replace a series of unreliable men. For Ethel Smyth and Vita Sackville-West (pages 102 and 117), two kindred spirits struggling to come to terms with the social and psychological consequences of their attachments to other women, their relationship with their beloved dogs Marco and Martha seem to have represented a depth of emotional involvement and provided the stability and constancy that they were unable to find elsewhere. To the Duke and Duchess of Windsor (pages 126–7), childless and exiled in a foreign country, the ever growing retinue of pugs must have constituted some sort of substitute for the family they never had. And what is one to make of the great ballerina Anna Pavlova and her swan Jack, whose amorous cavortings would have seemed indecent in any other animal (page 111)?

It was the dashing poet Lord Byron who was perhaps first

Fig. 10. Sir Walter Scott, 1st Bt, by Sir William Allan, 1831. Oil on board, 813 x 635mm. NPG 321

responsible for giving public respectability to such romantic attachments. Newly imported Newfoundland dogs such as his beloved Boatswain had begun to achieve something of a legendary status for their life-saving exploits during the Napoleonic Wars. When Boatswain died after a fit in 1808 at the age of five, the poet poured out his grief in misanthropic verse: 'To mark a friend's remains these stones arise; I never knew but one, and *here* he lies' – and then arranged for an elaborate monument with a lengthy panegyric to rise at Newstead Abbey, his ancestral home. Boatswain and Sir Walter Scott's deerhound Maida rapidly set a fashion for Newfoundlands and deerhounds that was quickly taken up by Queen Victoria and Prince Albert and their favourite painter, Landseer. The Victorian court seems to have considered it far too frivolous to include dogs in any formal portrait; indeed none ever appears in any portrait by the principal court painter, Franz Xaver Winterhalter.

The Royal Collection is nevertheless full of informal family groups and hundreds of portraits of dogs by Landseer and others, and proves Queen Victoria to have been one of the most enthusiastic dog-owners ever (fig. 11). She writes about them in her diaries and letters in exactly the same terms in which she writes about her family, although it was possibly only her King Charles spaniel Dash and Prince Albert's greyhound Eos who received the full Boatswain honours. The many paintings, photographs and the detailed documentation provided by the royal kennels make it possible to trace not only individual animals but also the changing fashions for different breeds that rapidly filtered down through the rest of society. In the 1870s and 1880s, the deerhounds are replaced by

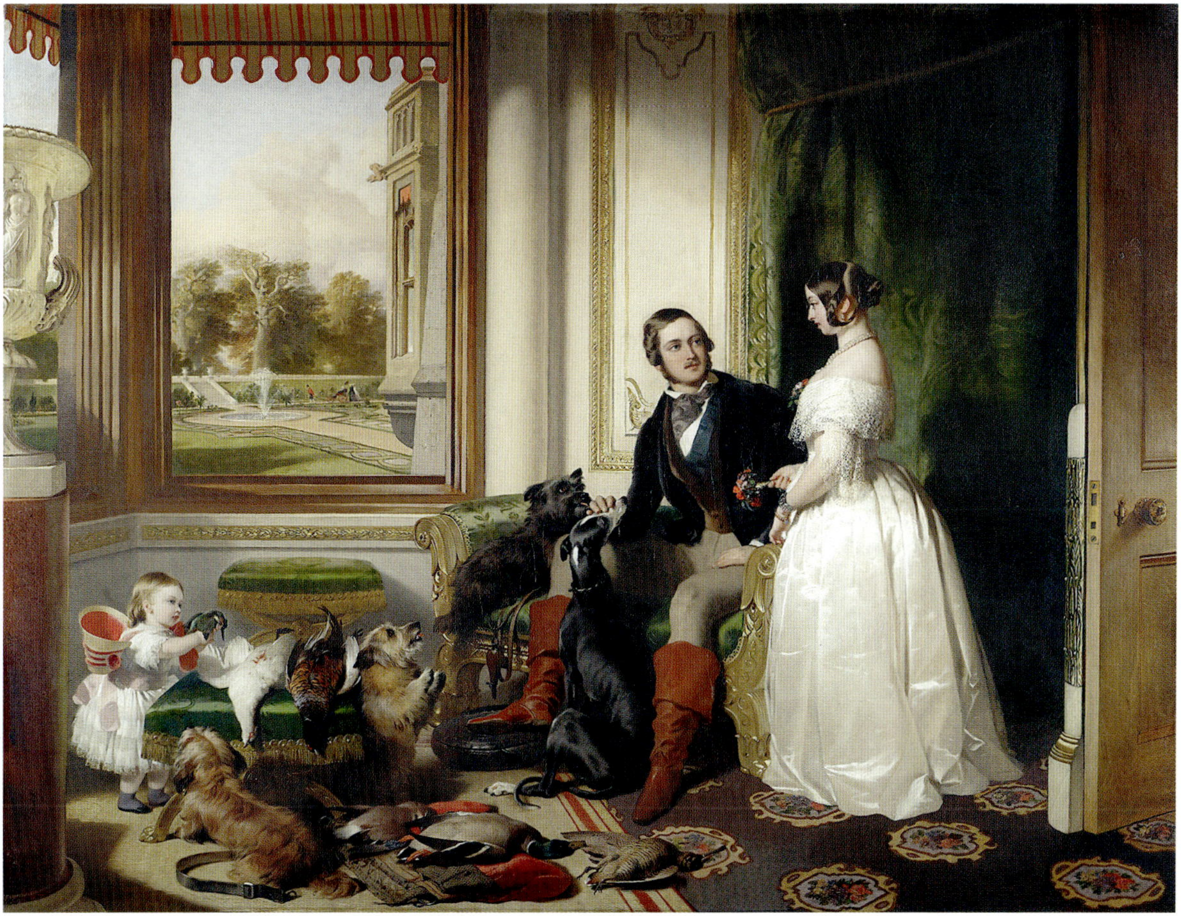

Fig. 11. *Windsor Castle in Modern Times*: Queen Victoria, Prince Albert (with Eos) and Victoria, Princess Royal, by Sir Edwin Landseer, 1841–3. Oil on canvas, 1134 x 1443mm. The Royal Collection © Her Majesty the Queen

border collies (page 96), the toy spaniels firstly by Skye terriers (the Scottish influence again) then by dachshunds and fox terriers and finally by Pomeranians. It was the little Pomeranian Turi whose company Victoria requested as she lay dying.

Her daughter-in-law Alexandra favoured the new oriental breeds, the Pekinese and Japanese Chin (page 105), and borzoi briefly replaced the royal greyhounds and deerhounds. Edward VII, a keen shooting man, and his son George V popularised Clumber spaniels, and Edward was devoted to his fox terrier Caesar, a breed first given to him by his mother in the 1870s (page 107). George VI and his family's devotion to the Welsh corgi brought a whole new perspective to the Royal Family's reputation as dog-lovers (page 137). Royal influence on fashion is perhaps no longer as powerful as it once was. The royal corgis singularly failed to set a fashion, except perhaps for a brief period in the 1950s, and Jack Russells and bull terriers had been popular for many years before being taken up by their royal owners. Fashions are now more likely to be set by modern advertising. It can be no coincidence that two of the most recent dogs to appear in portraits in the National Portrait Gallery are Labrador retrievers (fig. 12 and page 139), not only one of the most popular breeds as a family pet in the British Isles but also the stars of one of the most successful advertising campaigns of the last few decades for, of all things, a well-known brand of toilet paper.

Cats have been immune to fashion in almost every way and continue to maintain their place in the household much as they have always done. Whether it is their relative independence compared to dogs or their long association in the human mind with femininity, the message conveyed by the inclusion of a cat in a portrait will always remain subtly different from that of a dog. Perhaps something of the old superstitions still remain, but after five hundred years of British portraiture, it is still unthinkable, for example, to imagine a portrait of a monarch or a prime minister with a cat. Downing Street may have had its Humphrey, but a prime minister has a dog (fig. 12). The image of the dog as loyal, watchful, upright and the servant of man continues to live on in people's minds unscathed.

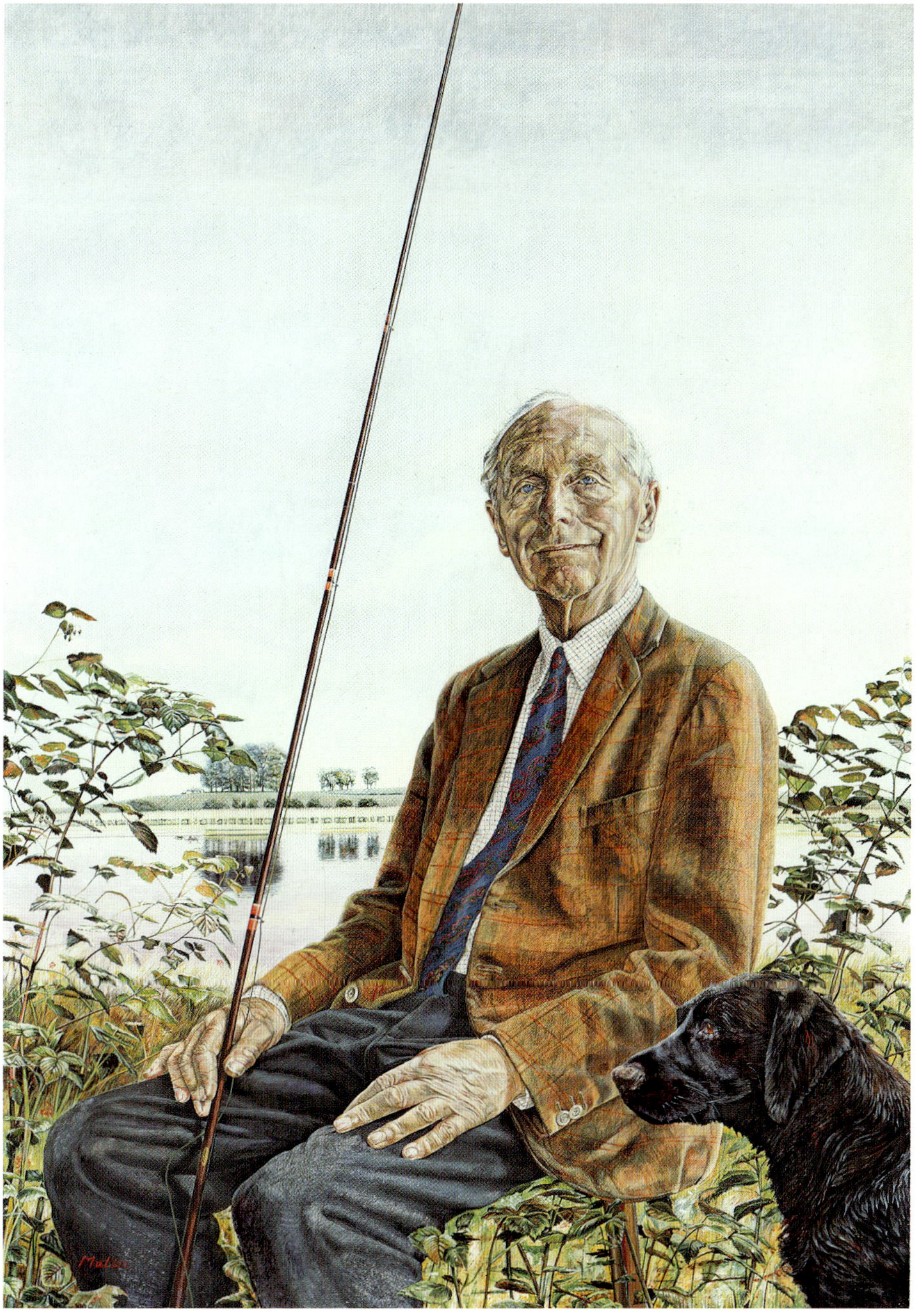

Fig. 12. Alexander Frederick Douglas-Home, Baron Home of the Hirsel by Suzi Malin, 1980. Tempera on panel, 1188 x 756mm. NPG 5367

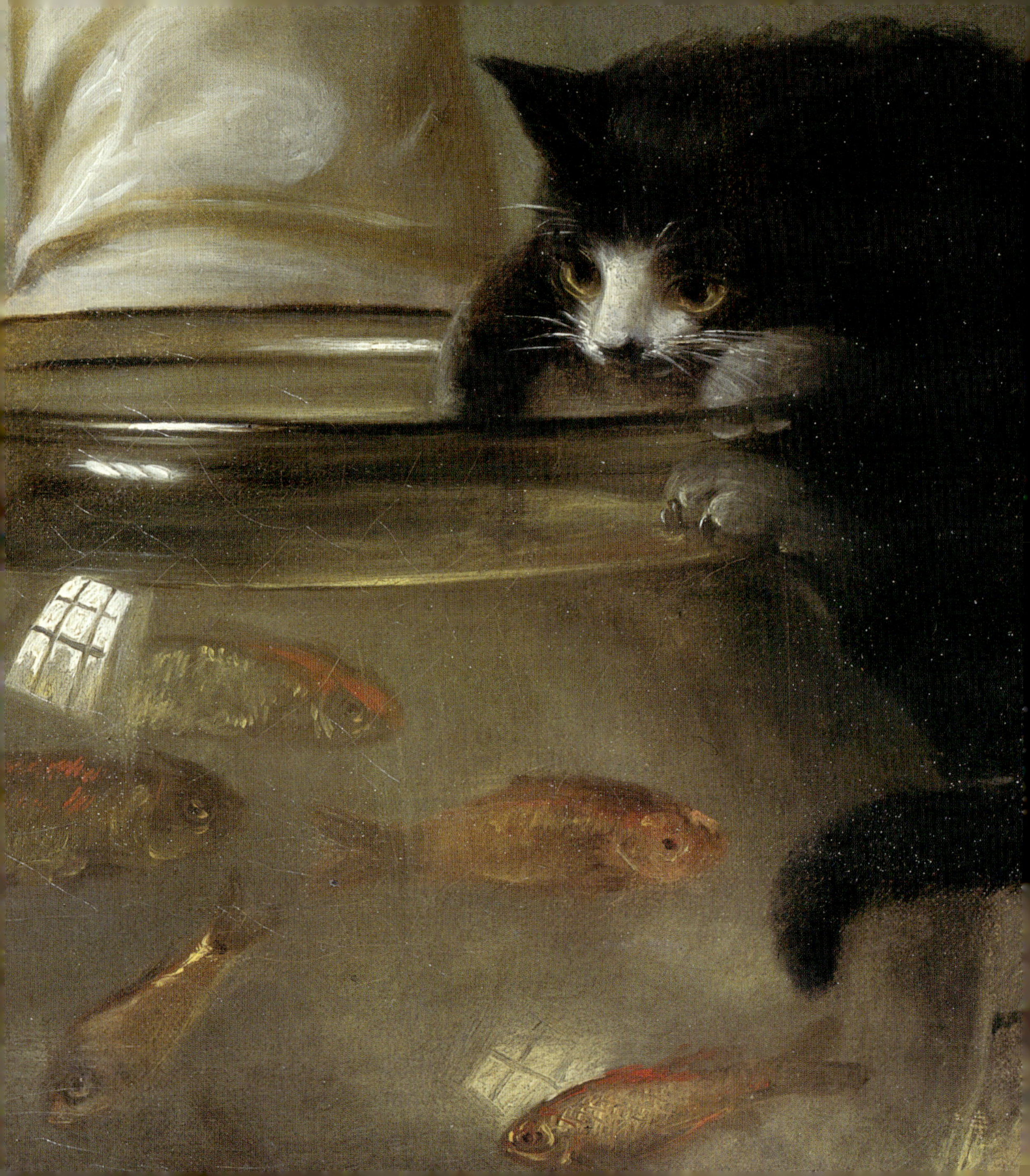

Pets *in* Portraits

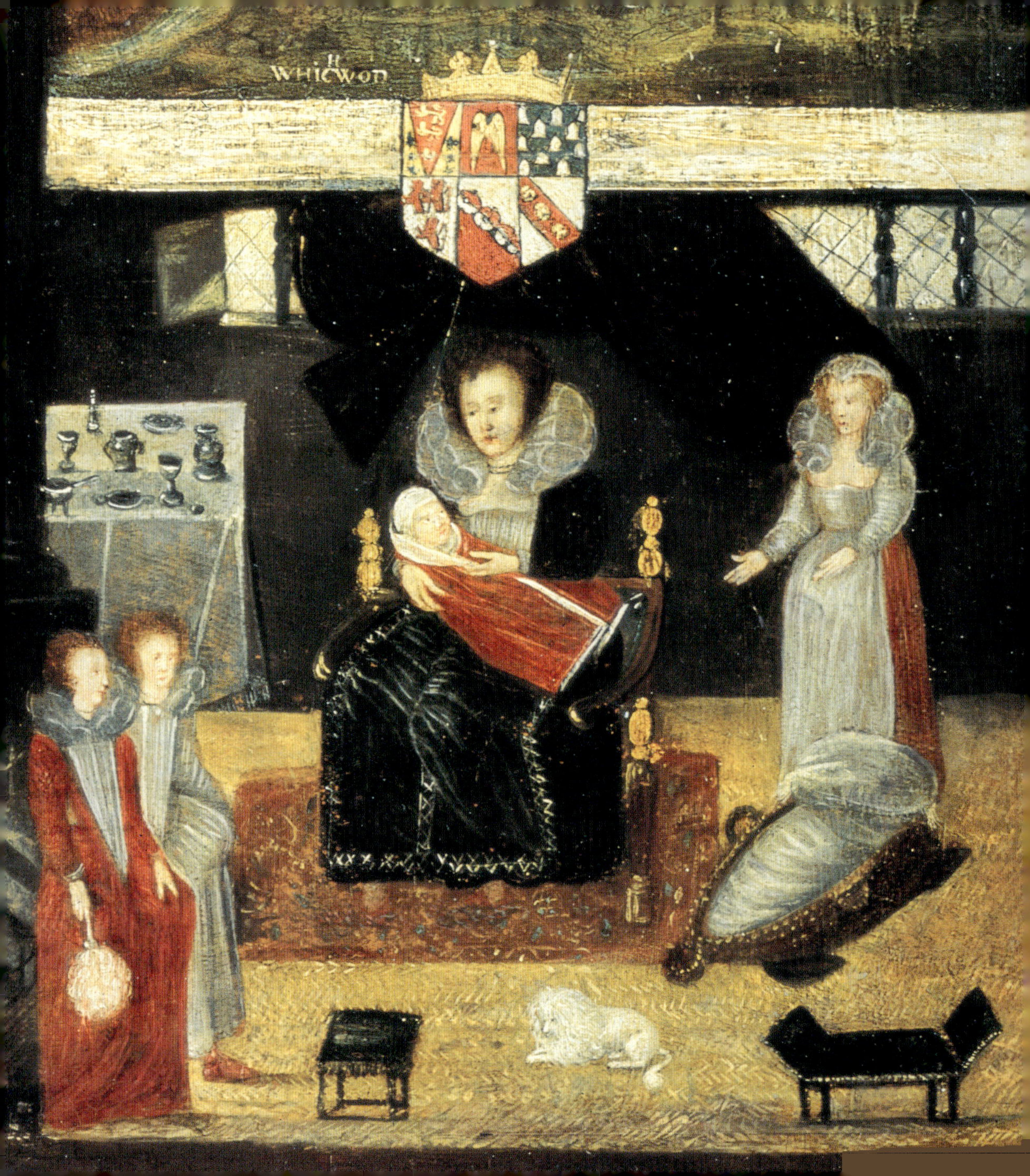
H
WHICWOD

SIR HENRY UNTON

Unknown artist, c.1596

Commissioned by his widow, Dorothy, this remarkable painting tells the life story of Sir Henry Unton, an Elizabethan soldier and diplomat who died during a mission to France.

The story begins at the bottom right, where after entering a house through the porch, the first scene portrays Sir Henry's early infancy. His mother, who like the rest of the important figures in the painting is portrayed larger than the other women in the room, was Lady Anne Seymour, niece of Henry VIII's Queen, Jane, and widow of the executed Earl of Warwick. This family connection with the highest in the land would have been of great importance to Unton's widow, and his father, Sir Edward, a mere country gentleman, makes no appearance in the painting at all. All the women in the room, including the nurse on the right and the two lady relatives on the left, wear costume of the date of Unton's death, rather than the late 1550s when Sir Henry was born.

At the foot of the cradle, lying on the woven rush matting between the stool and the settee, is a little white dog. With its shaggy mane and shaved body, it is probably one of the now rare little lion dogs, a breed that was popular throughout the courts and great houses of fifteenth- and sixteenth-century Europe. Unton himself could well have brought back a dog like this as a present for his wife from his first diplomatic mission to France in 1592. Far from being excluded from the bedrooms and ladies' chambers of the time, such dogs would have been positively welcomed in the belief that they would attract both fevers and parasites away from their owners to themselves. Indeed, it is documented that when Sir Henry was dying, the doctor sent by Henry IV of France to attend to him prescribed live pigeons to be placed on his sores for precisely this purpose.

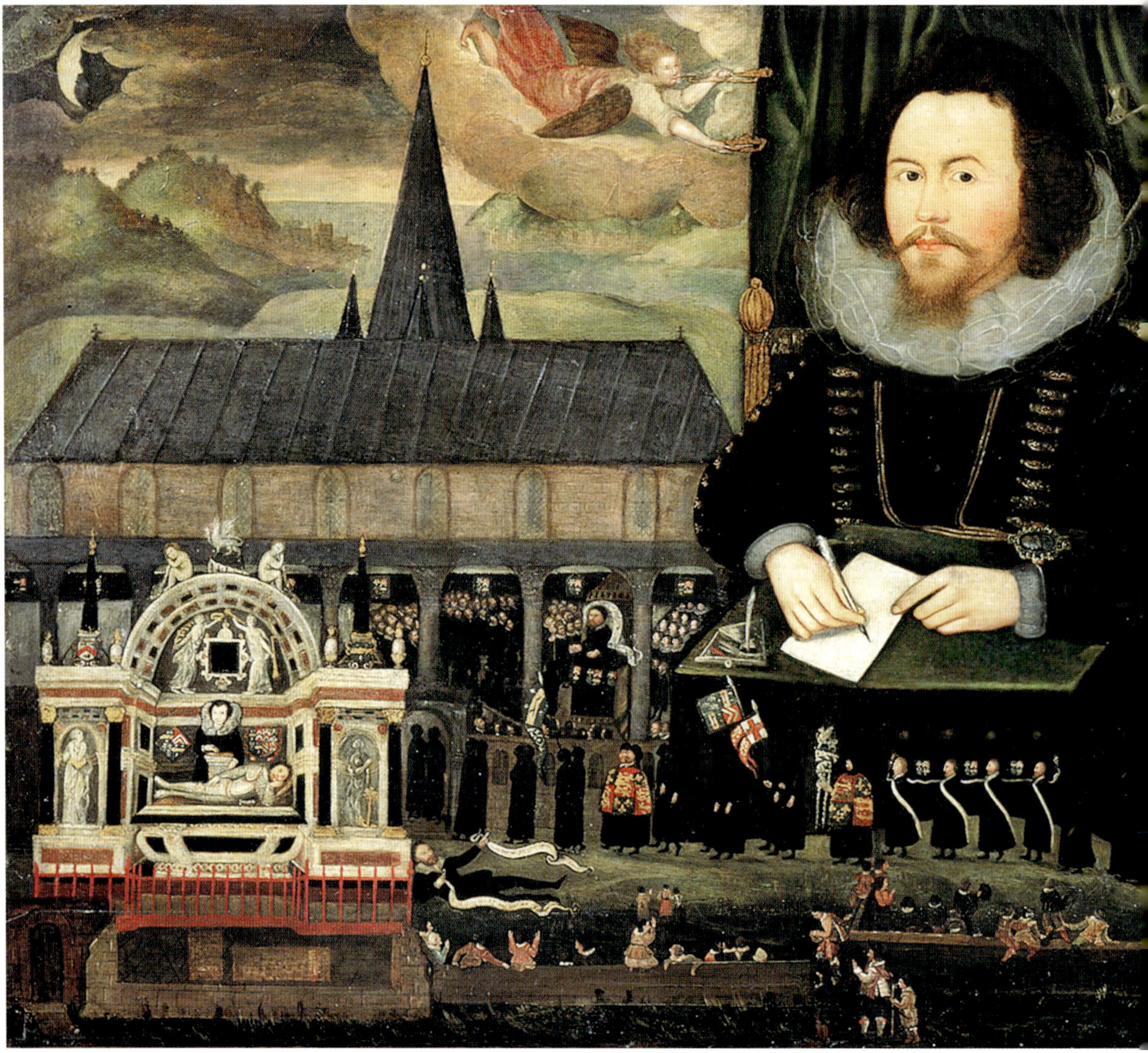

Sir Henry Unton (c.1558–96) by an unknown artist, c.1596. Oil on panel, 740 x 1632mm. NPG 710

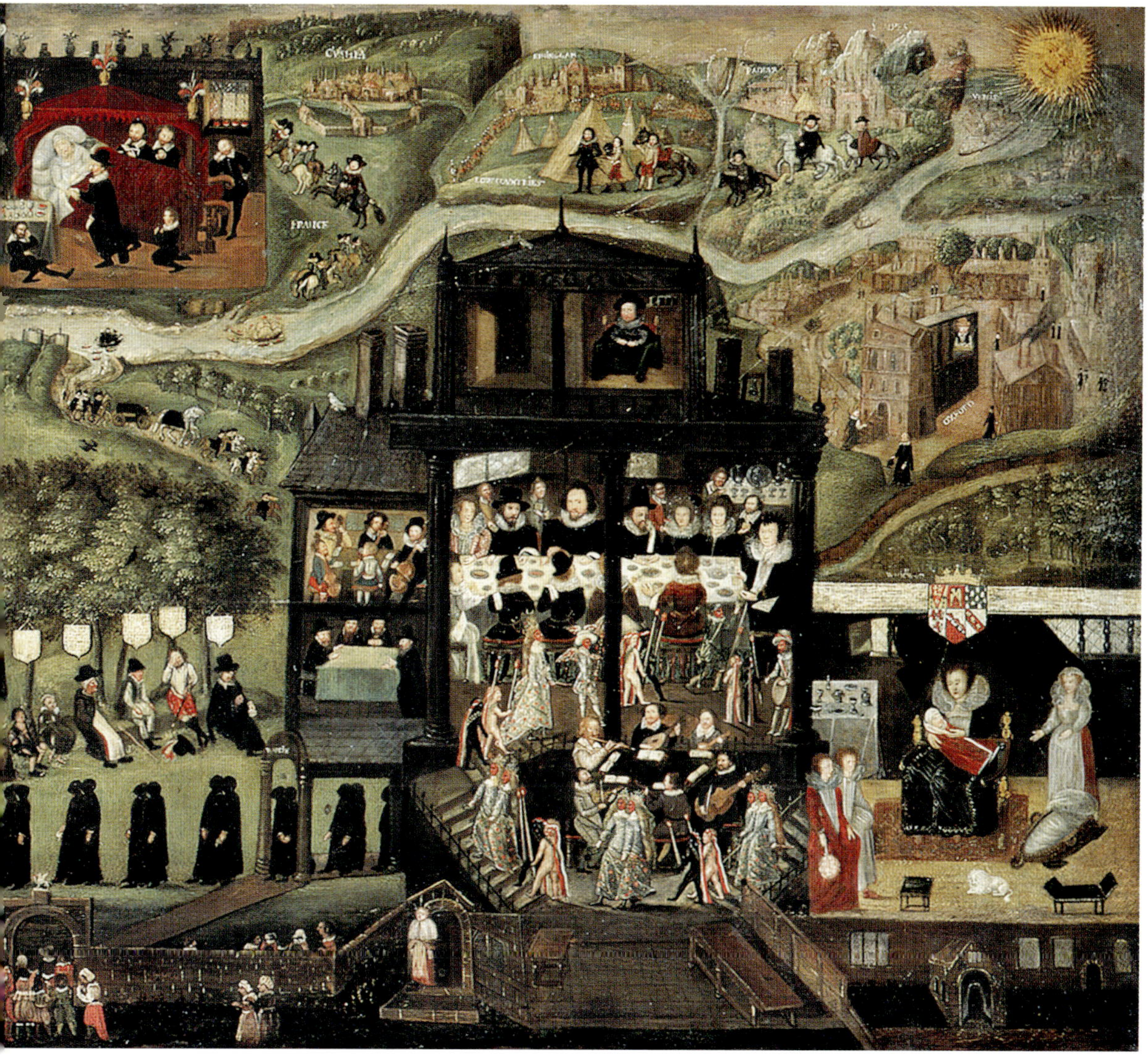

KING CHARLES II AS A BABY

Unknown artist, 1630

This larger-than-life portrait of the infant heir of Charles I is probably a painting commissioned by his mother, Queen Henrietta Maria, to send to her family in France. She wrote to a friend, Mme de Saint-Georges: 'I will send you his portrait as soon as he is a little fairer; for at present he is so dark that I am ashamed of him. ... He is so fat and so big that he is taken for a year old, and he is only four months.' A later letter implies that she had sent such a portrait to her mother, Marie de' Medici, and the inscription at the top of the picture is indeed in French and confirms that the Prince is four months old. His being dark is less apparent, though it is well documented, and his looks were almost certainly inherited from his Italian grandmother.

Despite the lack of any royal regalia, the portrait is self-evidently a piece of political propaganda, though the central role of the little puppy in the portrait is most unusual. Almost certainly painted life-size and occupying the focal point of the composition on the propped-up baby's lap, its symbolic function as the traditional emblem of loyalty to the lord and master is here overlaid with resonances of the subject's loyalty to and patronage from the heir to the throne. The dog's presence in the royal nursery as a magnet for the fevers and parasites that might otherwise afflict the child is, as has already been noted, not remotely unusual, and the dog would doubtless also serve where necessary as a hot-water bottle.

The liveliness and realism with which the dog is painted not only suggests that it may have been executed by a different artist from the rest of the painting, still

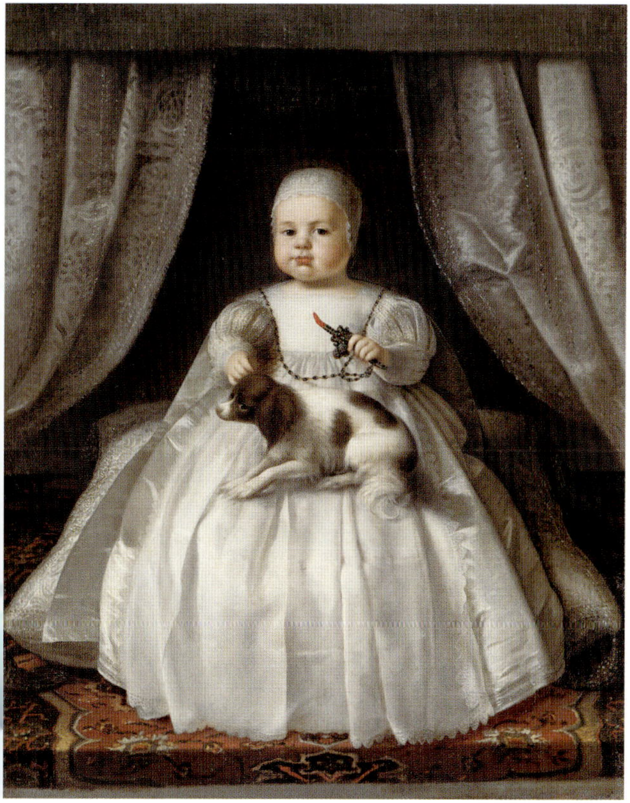

King Charles II (1630–85) as a baby by an unknown artist, 1630. Oil on canvas, 1207 x 933mm. NPG 6403

in the 'Jacobethan' tradition, but also allows us to identify it beyond doubt as one of the toy spaniels that seem to have been as much a feature of Charles I's court as they would later be of his son's. This still seems an amazingly prophetic touch, whether on the part of the Queen or of the artist, for these are the dogs for which the future Charles II became renowned, if not notorious, and which would later bear his name. Seen here as a baby playing with the dog's ear, in years to come the King would be the subject of grumbles from his ministers that, during government business, he whiled away the time by trifling with his spaniels.

FIVE CHILDREN OF KING CHARLES I

After Sir Anthony van Dyck, 1637

Van Dyck's sophisticated paintings of the court of Charles I must have come as a considerable culture shock to the majority of Britons who had never travelled in Europe. Painted only seven years after the stiff and hieratic portrait of Charles II as a baby (page 49), the young prince now dominates the centre of this elegant group of royal children, once more with a dog as accessory, though this time a rather spectacular mastiff. What cannot be seen in this reduced copy of the original full-length painting in the Royal Collection is yet another toy spaniel bouncing into the picture, as they do in almost all of Van Dyck's groups of the Royal Family.

The mastiff, while providing the usual symbol of loyalty and fidelity, nevertheless by its overwhelming presence and size seems also to suggest a symbol of power and perhaps of protection for its younger charges. The mastiff not only had been a guard dog since Roman times but was also the most common dog for the then hugely popular sports of bear- and bull-baiting, which had made even as well known a philanthropist as Edward Alleyn, founder of Dulwich College, immensely rich. He was empowered as Master of the Royal Game of Bears, Bulls and Mastiff Dogs to requisition any mastiffs he chose; as a result, by the end of James I's reign they had become something of an endangered breed. The mastiff's presence here, as well as reflecting Charles I's passion for baiting, may also by now have been something of a status symbol.

Charles II by contrast showed little interest in this cruel sport and will

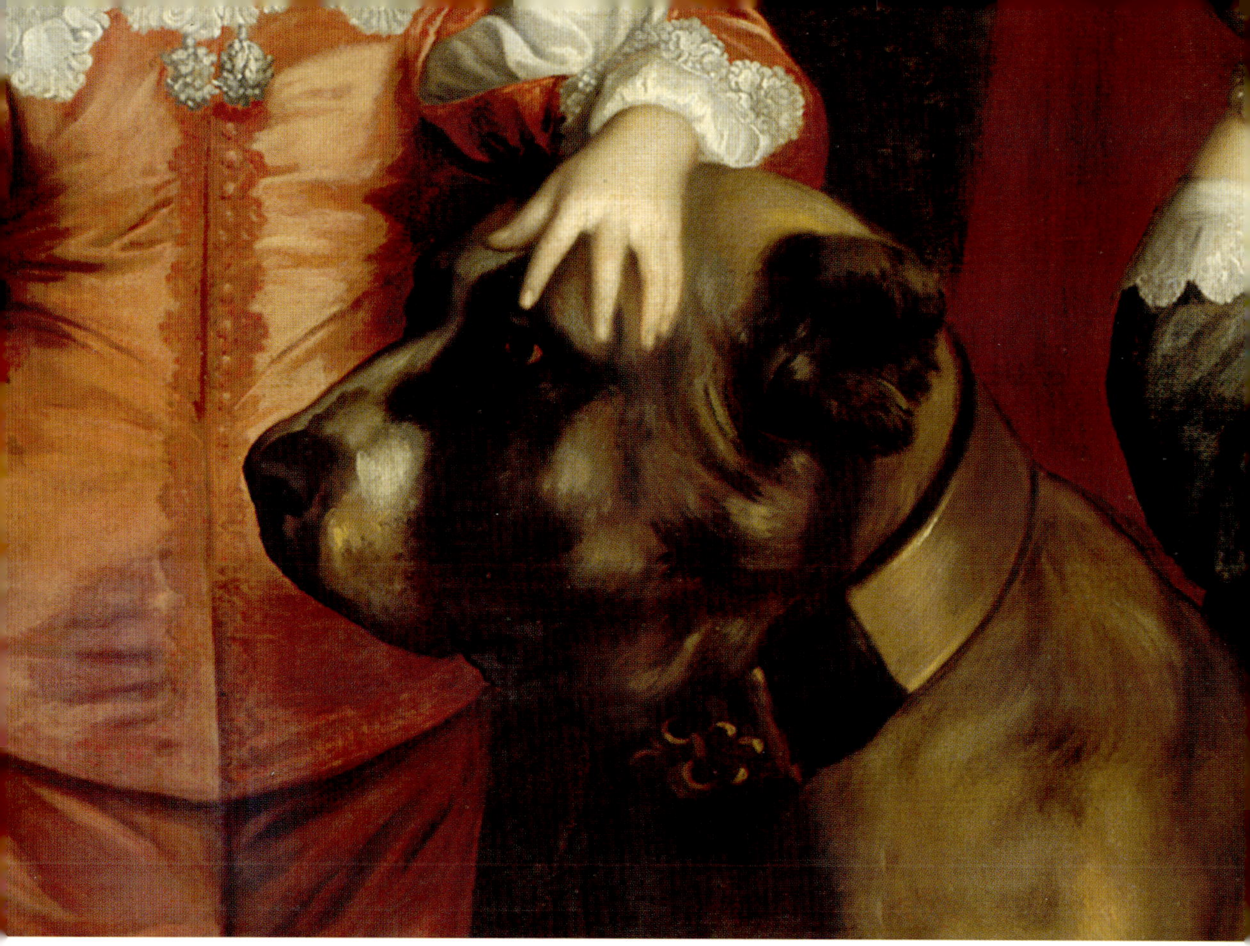

always be remembered for the spaniels that bear his name. In 1662, the Serjeant of Hawks was paid 20 pence a day for walking the King's spaniels and £7 for a suitable livery. The story is told, much like those in currency about today's royal corgis, of a loyal gentleman who was bitten by one of the spaniels and exclaimed, 'God bless your Majesty! But God damn your dogs!' In 1685, Bishop Burnet was shocked by the fact that even as the King lay dying, the royal bed was, as usual, alive with yapping and whimpering spaniels.

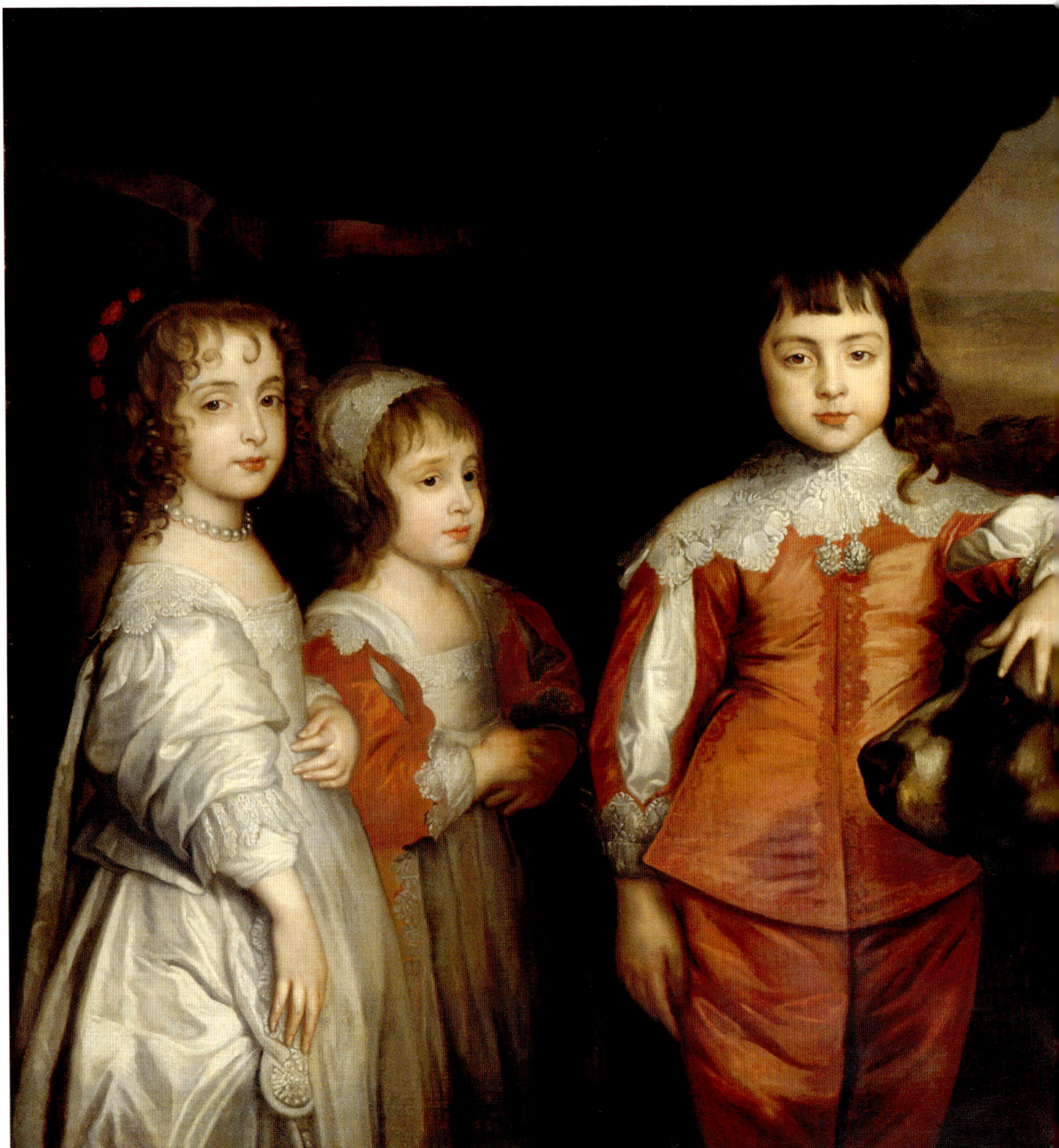

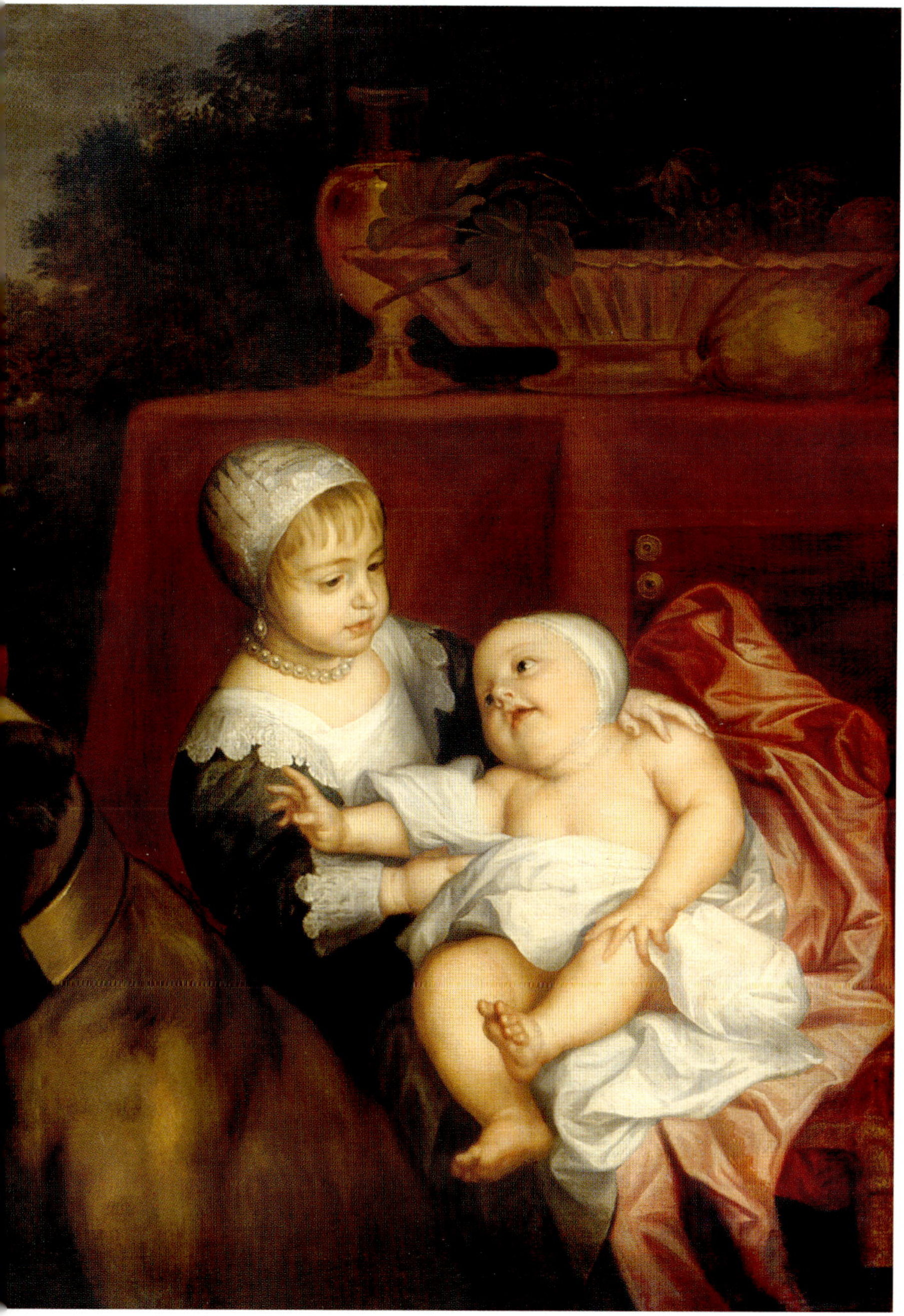

Five Children of King Charles I
after Sir Anthony van Dyck,
1637. Oil on canvas,
895 x 1762mm. NPG 267

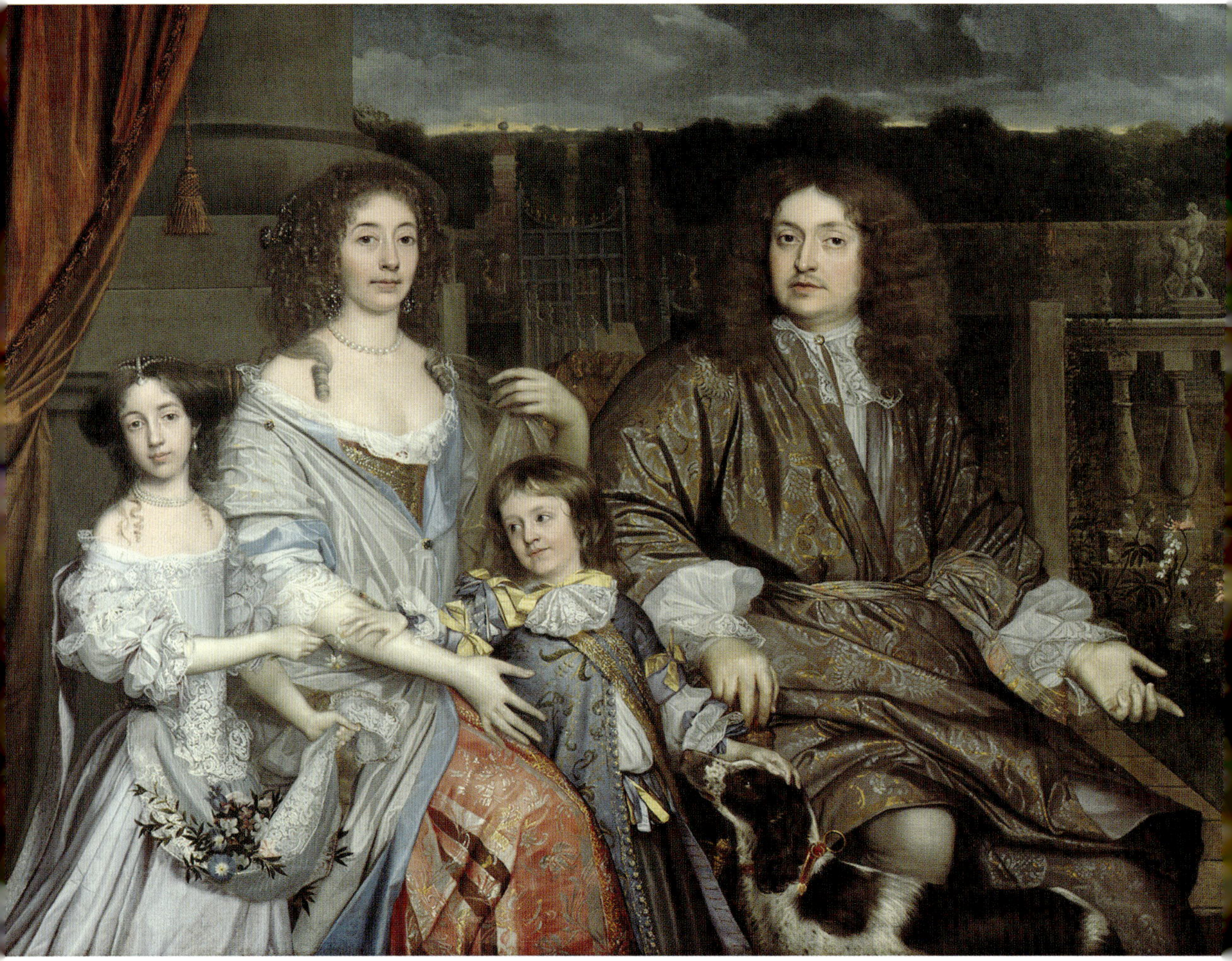

Sir Robert Vyner (1636–88) and his family by John Michael Wright, 1673. Oil on canvas, 1448 x 1956mm. NPG 5568

SIR ROBERT VYNER AND HIS FAMILY

John Michael Wright, 1673

Sir Robert Vyner was an extremely wealthy goldsmith and banker, whose constant favours to the newly restored Charles II (he made and presented the regalia used at the Coronation in 1661) not only put him on an intimate footing with the King but also eventually brought about his financial ruin. This opulent but rather touching family group was painted the year before he became Lord Mayor of London, marking the occasion with one of the most lavish banquets yet seen. It was only natural that he should also use one of Charles's painters, the Scottish-born John Michael Wright, from whom he had been instrumental in commissioning other works.

The group includes (from right to left) Vyner himself, his only son, Charles, his wife, Mary, and his step-daughter from his wife's first marriage, Bridget. The portrait is a significant one in British painting and marks a provincial, more realistic and bourgeois development from its Van Dyck predecessors. The little boy's dog with its traditional symbolism of fidelity and obedience was a standard accessory for the family heir and is used here as a masculine counterpart to the flowers that his sister is holding. Spaniels of all sorts were popular in the seventeenth century and were used for flushing out game, particularly in connection with the gentlemanly sport of falconry. This one, apparently a predecessor of the modern springer spaniel, has an opulent collar and is undoubtedly a status symbol, indicating not only gentlemanly rank but also a country estate with hunting. The domestic bliss pictured here was not to last for long. Vyner's wife died the following year; in 1683 Vyner was declared bankrupt. The boy Charles died in 1688, and Vyner himself followed two months later, broken-hearted at the death of his only child.

MARY OF MODENA

William Wissing, c.1685

Daughter of the Duke of Modena, the 14-year-old Italian princess had already been married to James, Duke of York, by proxy before she came to England in 1673. Earlier and less formal portraits of her by Sir Peter Lely, her brother-in-law Charles II's court painter, significantly often show her with the House of Stuart's favourite dog, a toy spaniel. In 1685, on the accession of James II, she became Queen, and William Wissing, a Dutchman and former pupil of the now deceased Lely, undertook the Coronation portraits. This is one of a small series of more intimate and informal paintings that were based on the sittings for the Coronation portrait and were probably intended as gifts for friends.

The painting positively bristles with conventional symbolism: the rose for the Queen's beauty and virtue, the twining honeysuckle for her constancy and the dog for fidelity. Despite her husband James II's well-documented love of hunting and dogs (he is said to have given the order 'Save the dogs and Colonel Churchill' when the *Gloucester* with Churchill, the future Duke of Marlborough, on board went down off the coast of Norfolk in 1682), there is no similar evidence for Mary. The little dog seen here, however, seems very identifiable; indeed it is a bitch and looks like an Italian greyhound, perhaps crossed with another breed. Apart from providing an oblique reference to her homeland, it does seem possible that it may have been her own dog, possibly a present from a relative. That it is, nevertheless, also a symbol is made clear in another version of this painting, where its place is taken by a cockatoo, to which similar attributes of devotion were ascribed.

Mary of Modena (1658–1718) by William Wissing, c.1685. Oil on canvas, 1220 x 978mm. NPG 214

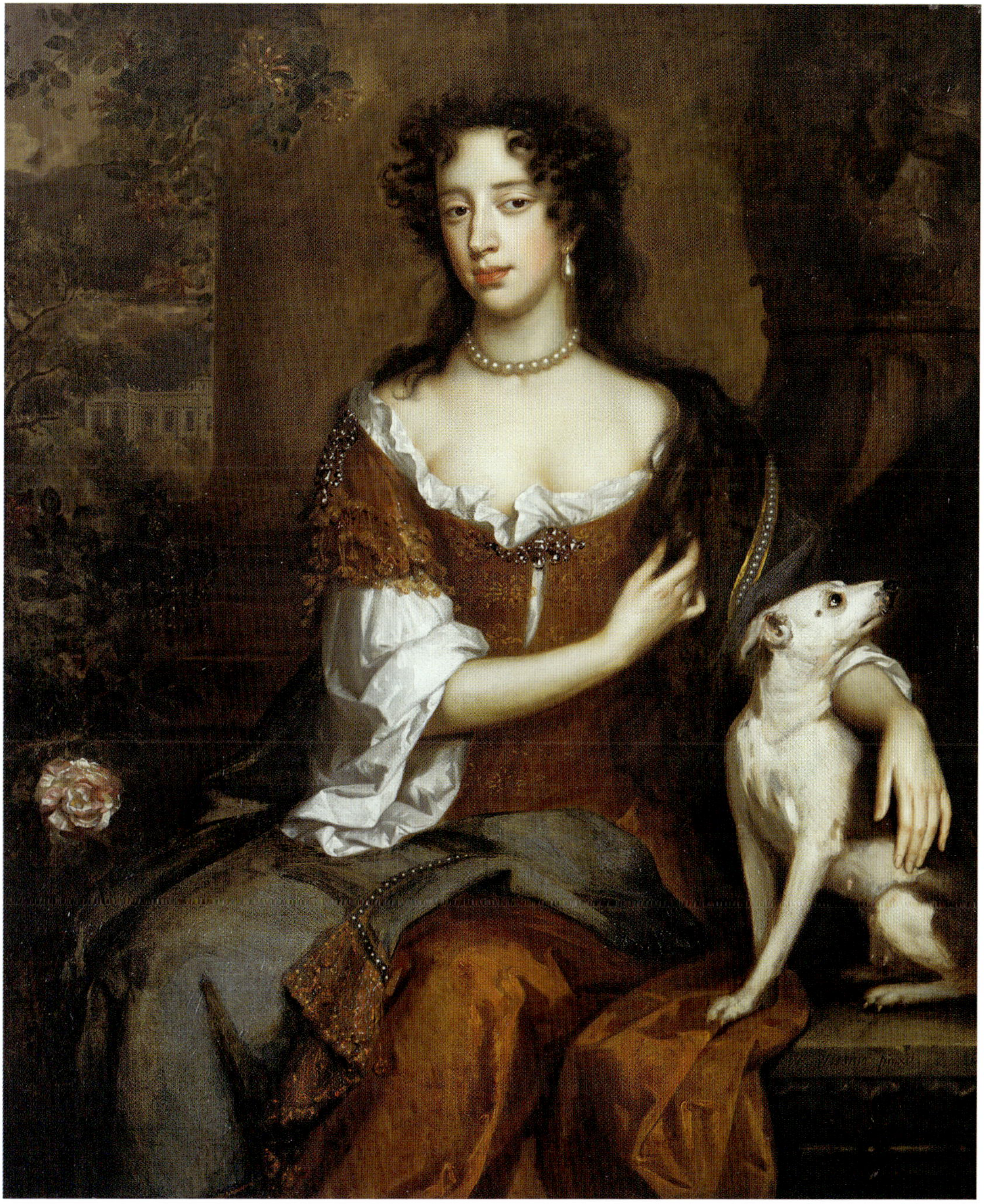

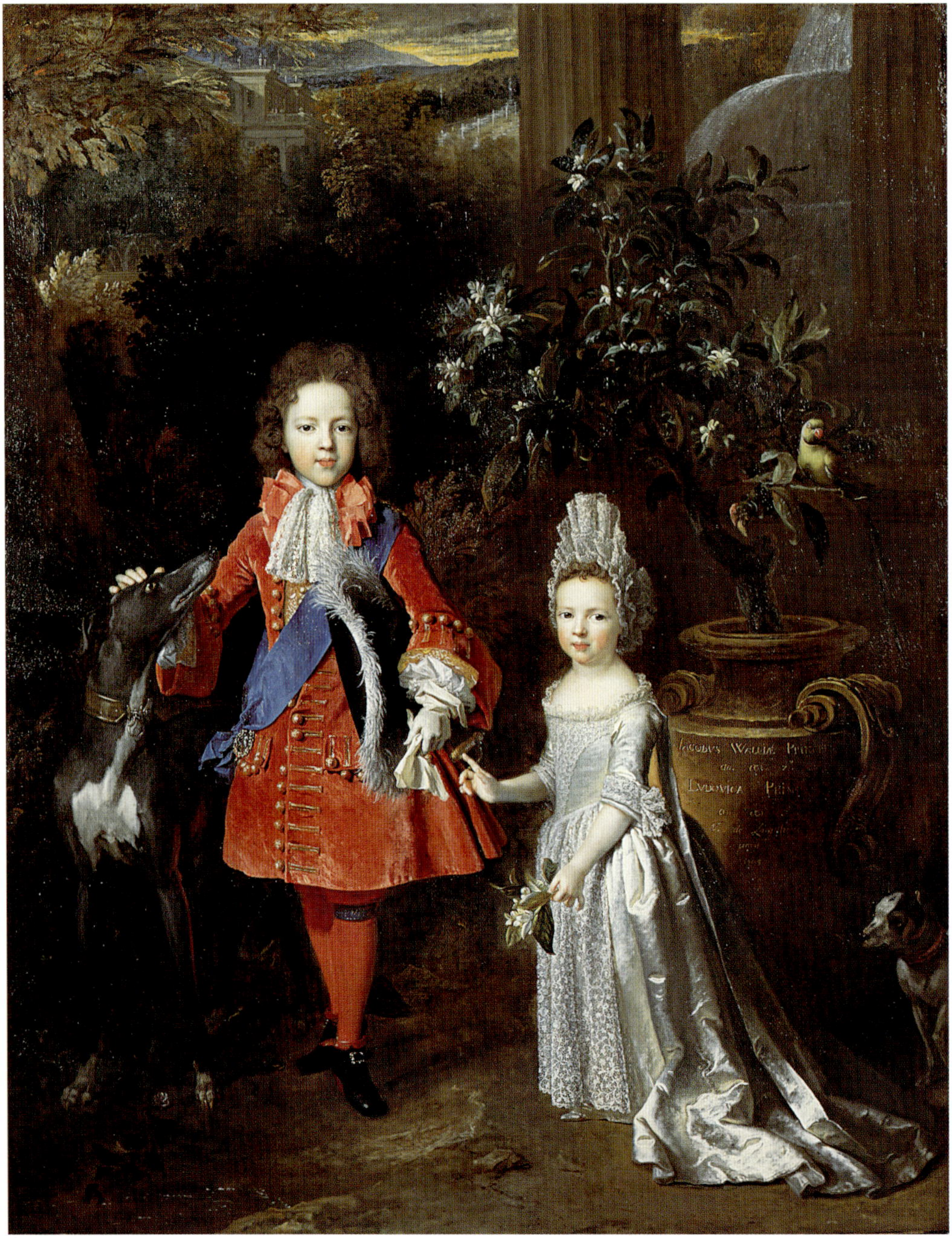

PRINCE JAMES FRANCIS EDWARD STUART AND HIS SISTER, LOUISA MARIA THERESA

Nicolas de Largillière, 1695

Both Charles II and James II had tried to persuade the brilliant French painter de Largillière to remain in Britain after he had done several court commissions for them, but with anti-Catholic feeling at its height, he had wisely chosen to return to France. Now, after the bloodless revolution of 1688 and living in exile at Saint-Germain-en-Laye under the protection of Louis XIV, James commissioned this portrait of his children from de Largillière as part of his ongoing campaign to re-secure for his family the British throne.

Like the earlier portrait of the baby Charles II (page 49), this is an unabashed piece of political propaganda, and like the portrait of the children's mother, Mary of Modena (page 57), it is full of the conventional symbolism of the times.

The innocence of the Stuart children in exile is indicated by the orange tree from which the little princess has plucked a sprig of blossom. She points to her brother, the rightful heir and future claimant to the British throne, loyalty to whom is symbolised by the magnificent greyhound standing over a twisting vine of morning glory between its feet, an emblem of constancy. She has her own faithful companions: the little male rose-ringed or ring-necked parakeet, which, like the orange tree and unbroken flow of the fountains behind her, symbolised her virginity and eligibility; seen emerging from the shadows behind her train, a small but sadly unidentifiable breed of dog.

The Prince's greyhound was one of the oldest and noblest of hunting dogs, its aristocratic looks, grace and intelligence complementing his royal status. But unless there is some hidden agenda, the symbolism of the orange tree might seem at best a little careless for it was the House of Orange and Prince William, now King of England, who were responsible for the current plight of the Stuart children.

Prince James Francis Edward Stuart (1688–1766) and his sister, Louisa Maria Theresa (1692–1712), by Nicolas de Largillière, 1695. Oil on canvas, 1928 x 1457mm. NPG 976

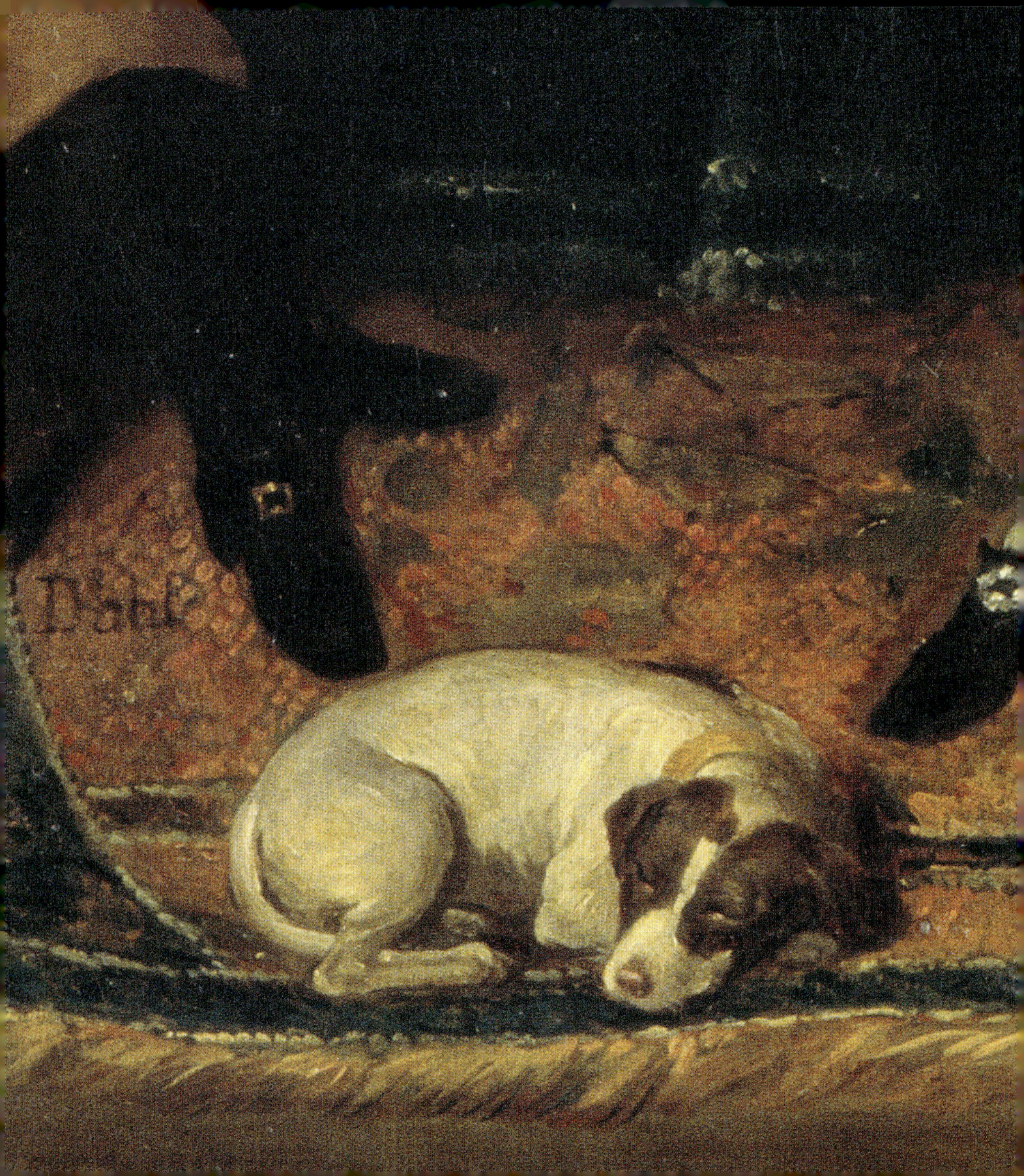

A CLUB OF ARTISTS

Gawen Hamilton, 1735

The man in the dark coat holding a book, on the left of this group of early eighteenth-century British artists, is the noted engraver and antiquary George Vertue, to whom we owe all we know about this picture and almost everything that is known about its artist, Gawen Hamilton. Vertue described the painting as a 'Conversation of Virtuosis that usually meet at the Kings Armes. New bond Street a noted Tavern'. It includes painters like Michael Dahl and John Wootton, architects like James Gibbs and William Kent and the sculptor John Michael Rysbrack. All the figures are named on the painting except the only one in working clothes, Hamilton himself, who is the gaunt figure in a cap on the right behind the bust. Born in Scotland around 1697, he came to London in about 1730 and became William Hogarth's chief rival as a painter of small-scale portrait groups like this one, known as conversation pieces. This probably explains Hogarth's absence from the painting, though in any case the rivalry was short-lived, for Hamilton died young two years later.

There is no evidence for ownership of what looks like a spaniel sleeping peacefully in the foreground, though Hamilton's stylistic trademarks include the almost invariable presence of a dog in the front of his portraits as well as the slightly rucked carpet, which appears to be not quite attached to the floor. It is tempting to suppose that the dog belonged to the ageing Swedish painter Michael Dahl, at whose feet it is sleeping, or even to Hamilton himself, though he stands a long way off. If identifiable at all, a more likely explanation, especially since the grandiose background seems most unlikely to represent a pub of any sort, is that it belonged to the landlord of the 'Kings Armes' and as such would have been instantly recognisable not only to everyone in the painting but also to all other habitués of that 'noted Tavern'.

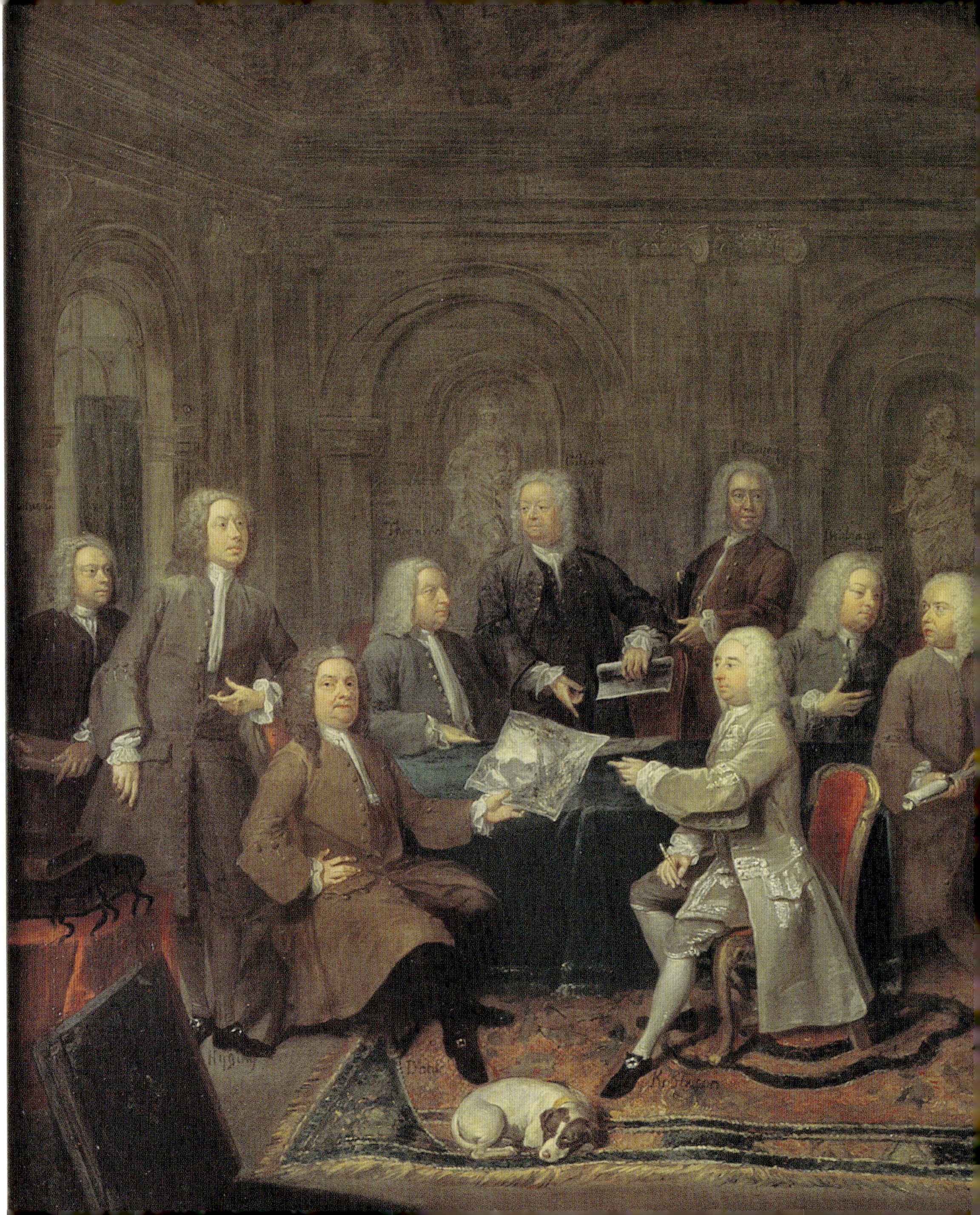

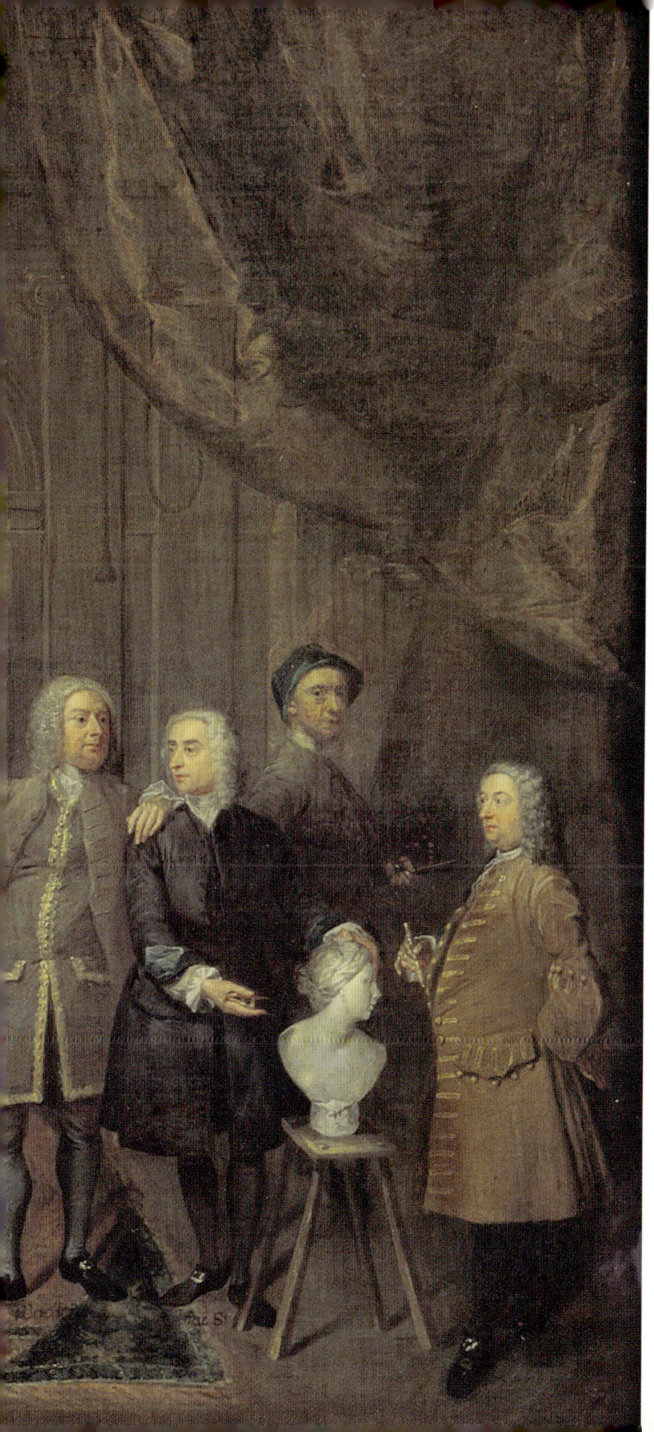

A Club of Artists by Gawen Hamilton, 1735.
Oil on canvas, 876 x 1115mm. NPG 1384

BURKAT SHUDI AND HIS FAMILY

Marcus Tuscher, c.1742

The foremost harpsichord-maker in Britain, Shudi came to this country from the Swiss canton of Glarus in 1718 and was soon a friend of Handel and a respected member of the musical and German-speaking circles in London. Portraits of his royal patrons, Frederick, Prince of Wales, and Princess Augusta, can be seen hanging on the wall behind, and his commercial success was such that he had recently been able to move to this comfortable new town house in Great Pulteney Street, Soho. This painting, by a visiting German artist, clearly seems intended to show both Shudi's professional and social standing and is an outstanding example of the newly fashionable conversation piece, popular with the new middle classes. His wife, Catherine, also from Glarus, is seen as a woman of leisure, reading and presiding over tea. His older son, Joshua, is pointing to the source of their well-being, the harpsichord and the business that he will eventually inherit. In fact, his father went into partnership with an apprentice, John Broadwood, and Joshua later became junior partner in Broadwoods, the great piano manufacturers.

The younger son, Burkat junior, being restrained by his mother, is holding what looks like a rusk, with which he has been teasing the pretty grey-and-white tabby, who is mewing in vain for this tasty treat. For centuries cats had been tolerated round the house as the most effective form of rodent control, but since medieval times they had acquired undeserved associations with witchcraft and had been seen as symbols of everything from Satan to lethargy and lust. Such considerations

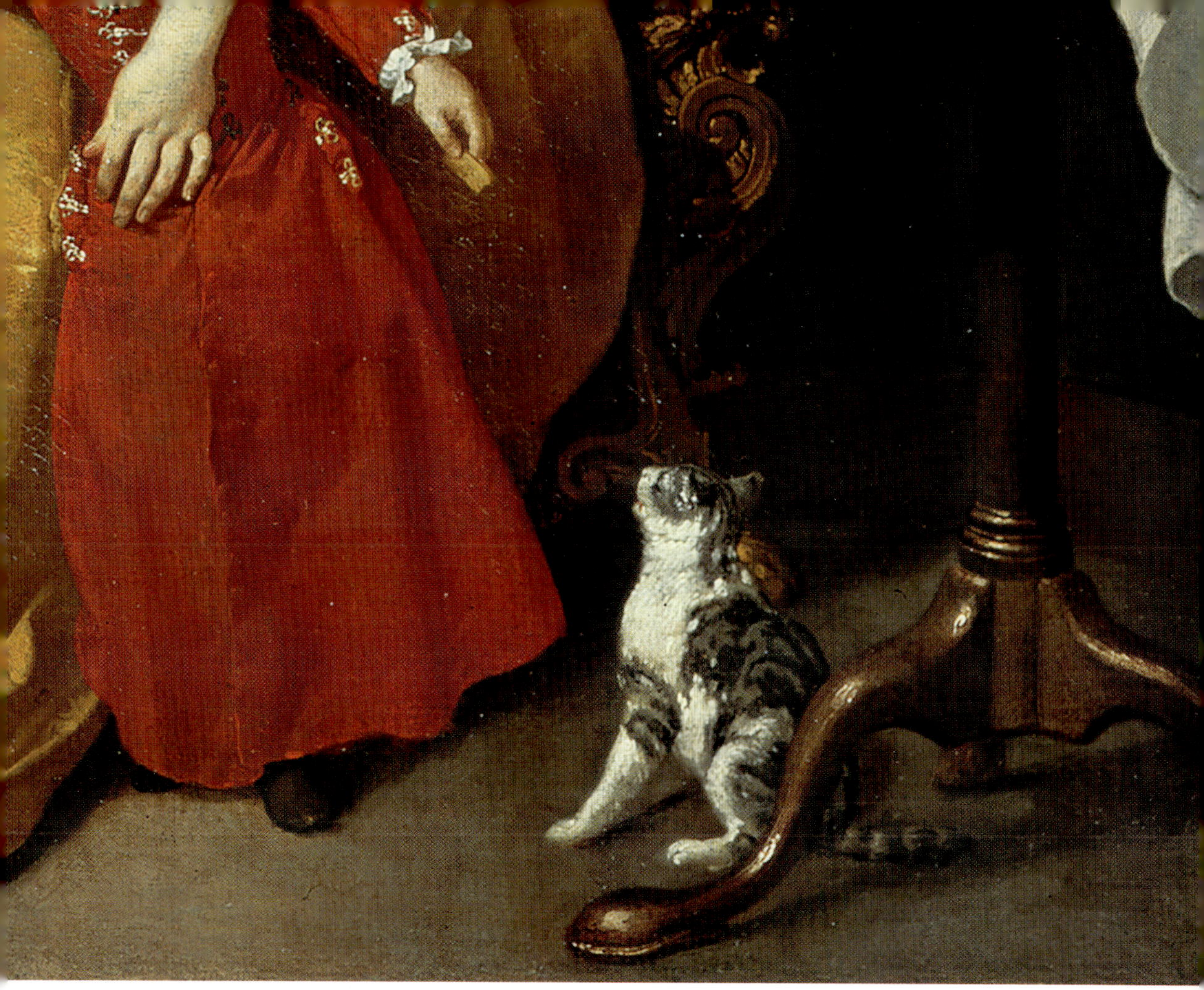

bore little weight in the more rational mood of the eighteenth century, and, as here, cats make their appearance in paintings as suitable playthings for children and symbols of civilised domesticity. For a successful professional family like the Shudis with no ambitions to be accepted as country gentlefolk, a cat was a far more suitable pet than a dog for city living.

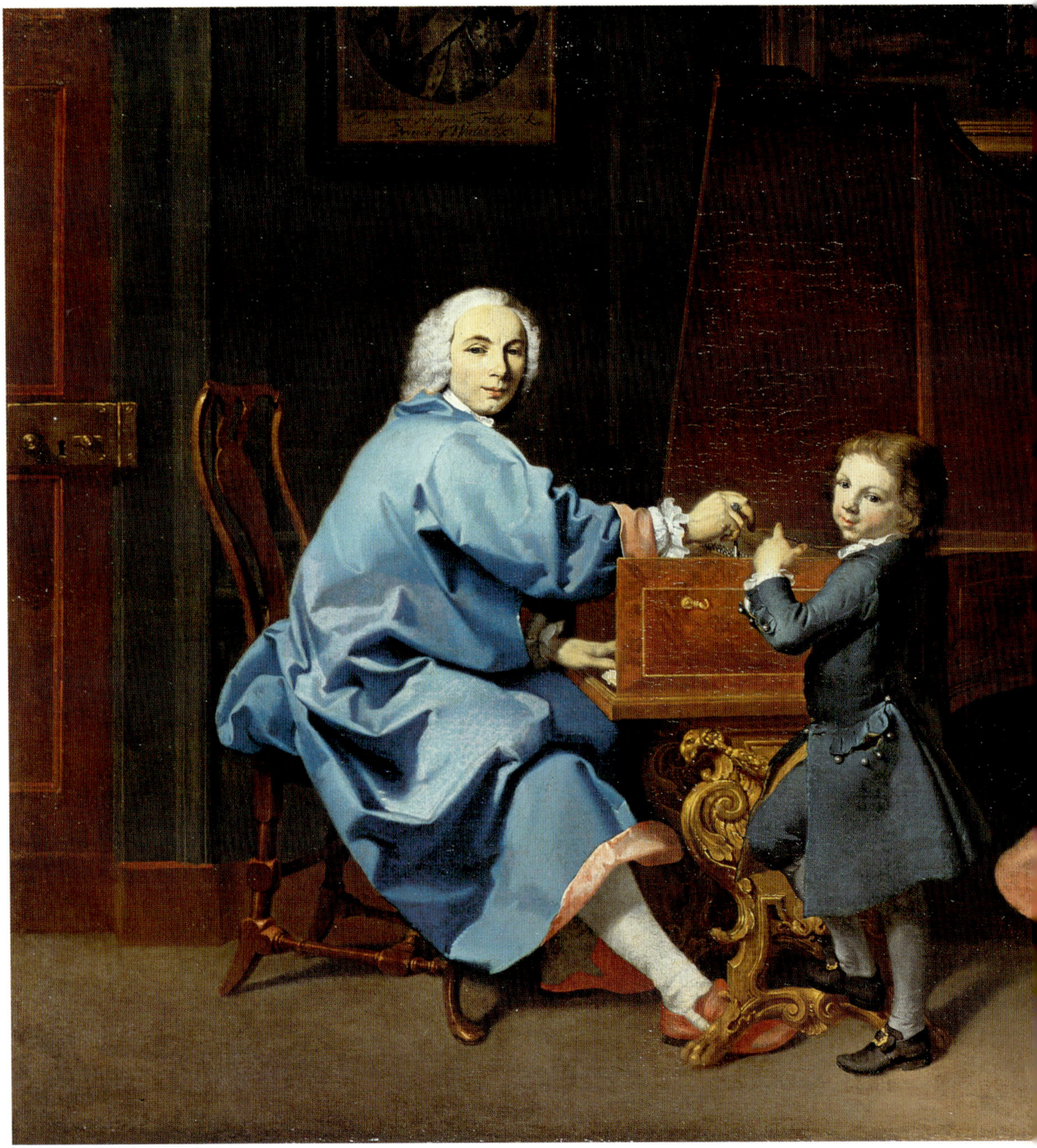

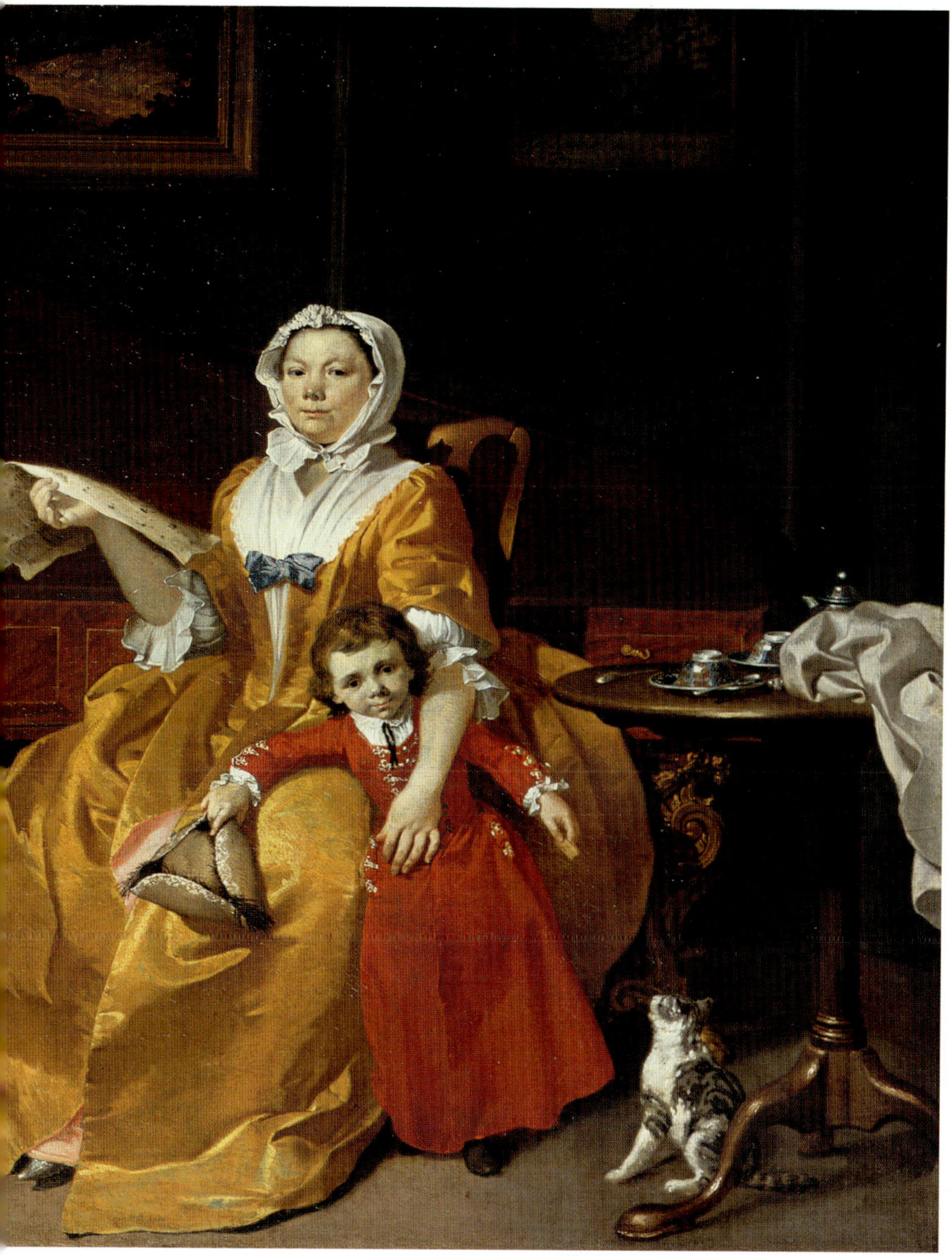

Burkat Shudi (1702–73) and his family by Marcus Tuscher, c.1742. Oil on canvas, 834 x 1415mm. NPG 5776

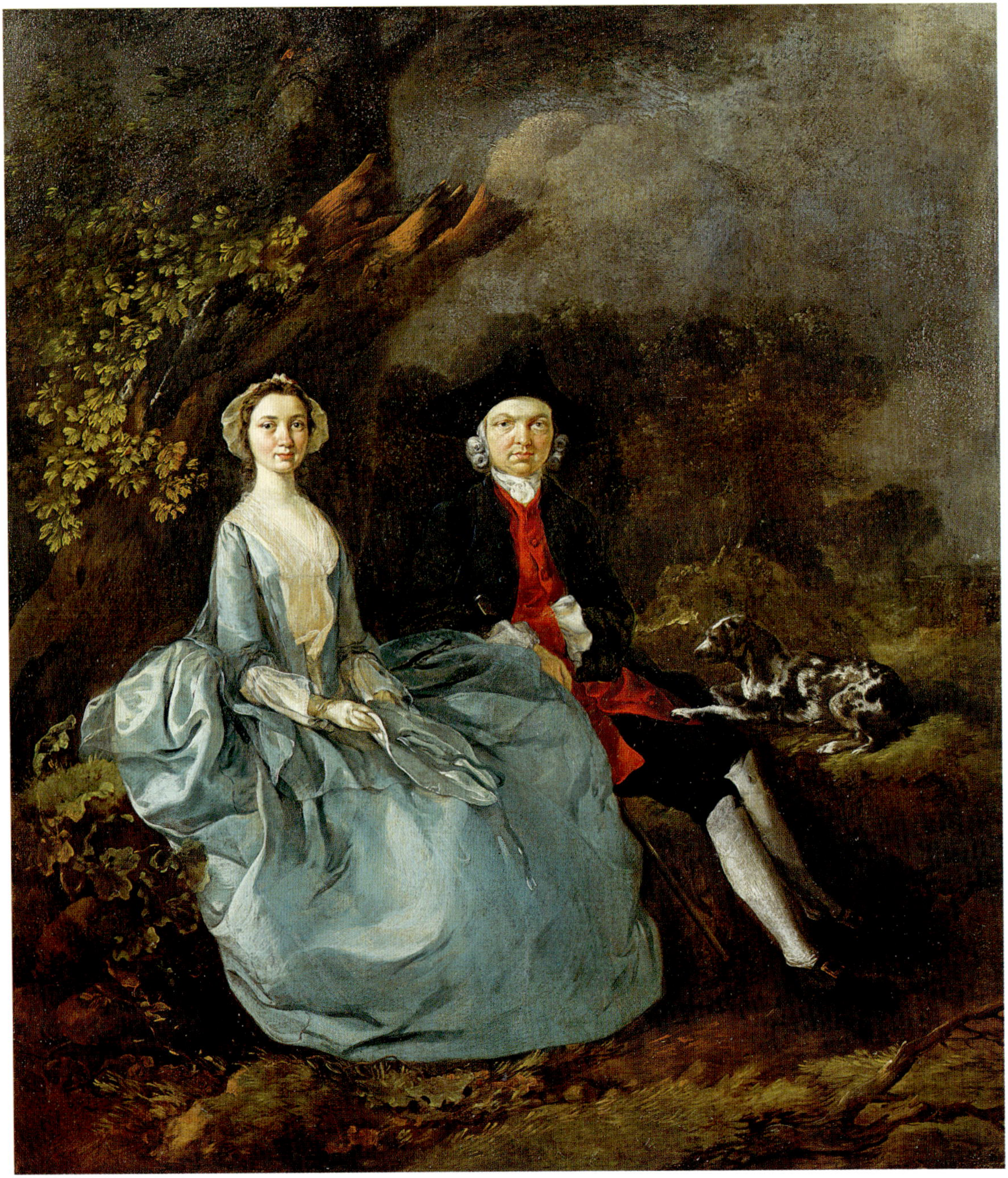

JOHN JOSHUA KIRBY AND HIS WIFE

Thomas Gainsborough, c.1751–2

Gainsborough met the Kirbys after he moved back to Suffolk in 1748, having both completed his apprenticeship and failed to make a living in London. Life in Ipswich was not much more profitable, and Gainsborough relied on local professional people for his few portrait commissions and for the even rarer sale of the evocative landscapes, rather Dutch in style, at which he was beginning to excel. Kirby was not only the author of an early illustrated book on Suffolk and of a well-known book on perspective but also ran a general painting business, with which Gainsborough probably helped him out. This portrait commission may well have cemented what was to become a lifelong friendship, to the extent that in the last weeks of his life Gainsborough gave instructions that he was to be buried next to Kirby in Kew churchyard.

It is possible to deduce from Gainsborough's paintings that he must have loved and owned dogs all his life. His earliest dated painting (1745) is of the magnificent white bull terrier Bumper, and although he only painted about half a dozen such 'portraits', including his own two little dogs *Tristram and Fox* (Tate Gallery), dogs constitute a significant element in many of his major portraits and 'fancy' pictures, especially in later works like *The Morning Walk* (fig. 9). In the early little self-portrait with his wife and daughter in the National Gallery, painted a few years before the Kirbys, the family's small spaniel drinks from a pool. The Kirbys' dog, here looking strangely out of scale and slightly disreputable – a spotty gun dog of some sort – seems designed to introduce a little light and shade into a difficult area of composition and may have been a later addition. Indeed X-rays reveal several changes of mind during the course of painting, including a large classical monument behind Kirby, which was later dispensed with.

John Joshua Kirby (1716–64) and his wife by Thomas Gainsborough, c.1751–2. Oil on canvas, 768 x 637mm. NPG 1421

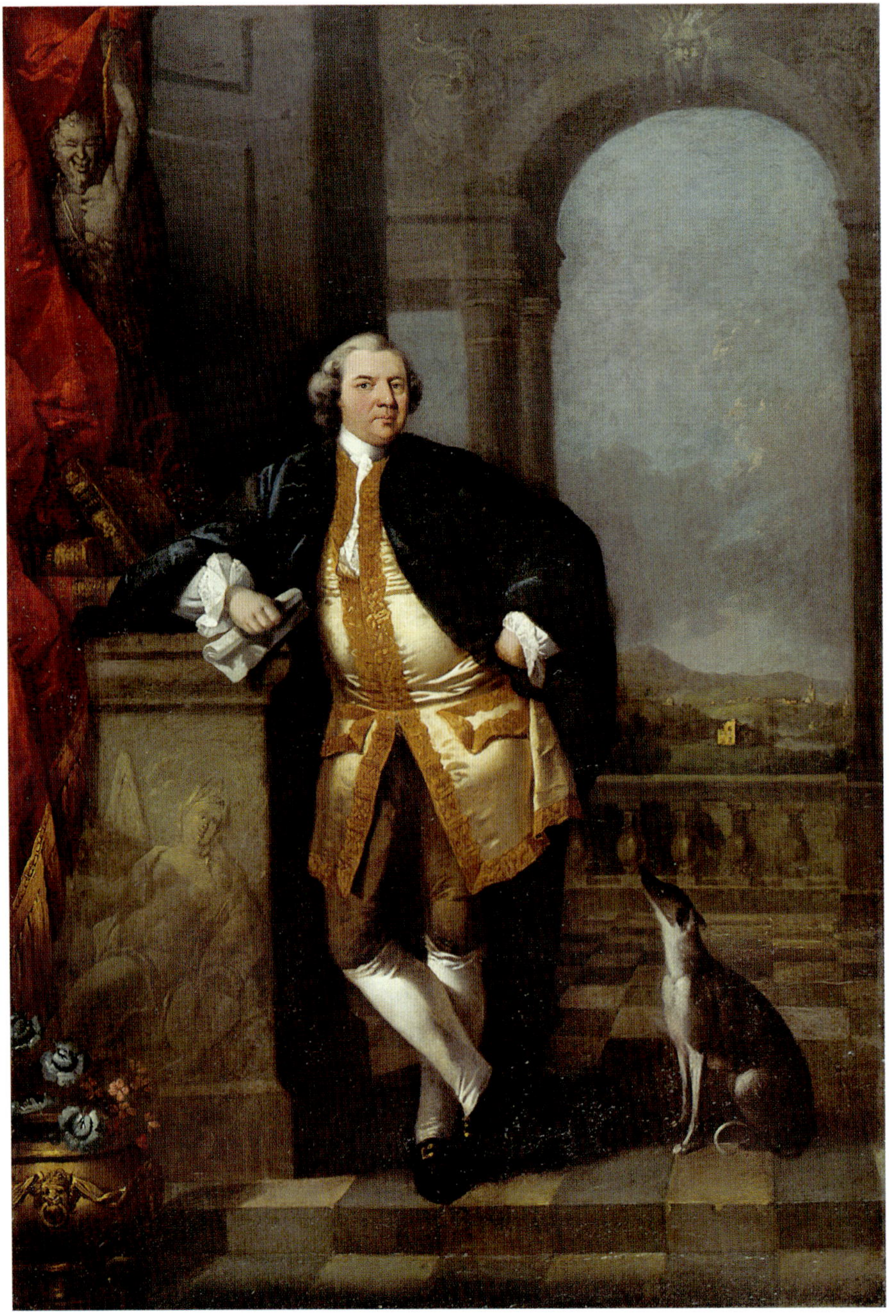

William Shenstone (1714–63)
by Edward Alcock, 1760. Oil on
canvas, 1508 x 997mm. NPG 263

WILLIAM SHENSTONE

Edward Alcock, 1760

'A large, heavy, fat man, shy and reserved with strangers,' William Shenstone was a poet from the Midlands and a bachelor. Of private means, he had inherited the estate of Leasowes near Halesowen from his guardian in 1745 and began what was in effect his life's work, laying out and beautifying the grounds. The Leasowes was to become in the words of his schoolfriend, Dr Johnson, 'a place to be visited by travellers and copied by designers', and Shenstone holds an important place in the history of British landscape gardening. Through the arch in the painting can be seen the village of Halesowen and the 'ruinated priory' that he had erected in the grounds.

Shenstone's *Letters* include detailed descriptions of his requirements for this portrait, which he had commissioned from a local artist. The relief of the water nymph on the pedestal was to represent the River Stour, 'which in some sort rises at The Leasowes'. The 'scarlet geranium' in the 'antique vase' would also reflect his interests, though it had to be supplied by a friend. 'The dog on the other side is my faithful Lucy, which you perhaps remember,' Shenstone says in a letter to his lifelong friend, the poet Richard Graves. In contrast to the outdoor pursuits usually implied by eighteenth-century portraits of one man and his dog, the classical allusions and the look of mute adoration on the face of the little greyhound imply a closer form of companionship. Lucy may well have outlived her master, for Shenstone died three years later.

CATHERINE 'KITTY' FISHER

Nathaniel Hone, 1765

When this portrait was exhibited anonymously at the Society of Arts, London, in 1765, the art critic of the newspaper *The Public Advertiser* observed: 'This is a portrait of a Lady *whose charms are well known to the town*. The Painter has ingeniously attempted to acquaint us with her name by a rebus upon Canvass.' In fact, the artist's punning clue, the 'rebus' of the kitten fishing, can scarcely have been necessary, for Kitty Fisher was not only one of the most celebrated beauties in the London of the late 1750s and early 1760s but was also a notorious courtesan.

The artist, the Dublin-born Nathaniel Hone, was not otherwise known for his wit, but the portrait bears all the hallmarks of the considerable charm he brought in particular to portraits of children, whom he often pictured with a favourite pet. The mischievous black-and-white kitten was in more ways than one a suitable metaphor for his subject here, and the image is laden with symbolism. With a certain naive innocence, Kitty had published a defence of her character in 1759, and the reflection in the goldfish bowl of the crowd of people watching through the window is a vivid comment on the sort of invasion of privacy from the media with which we are all too familiar today. The goldfish in themselves are unusual, possibly even making their first appearance in a European painting. They are believed to have been first introduced into Britain from China some seventy years before the date of this picture and were probably shipped in large glass bowls similar to this one.

Catherine 'Kitty' Fisher (d.1767) by Nathaniel Hone, 1765. Oil on canvas, 749 x 622mm. NPG 2354

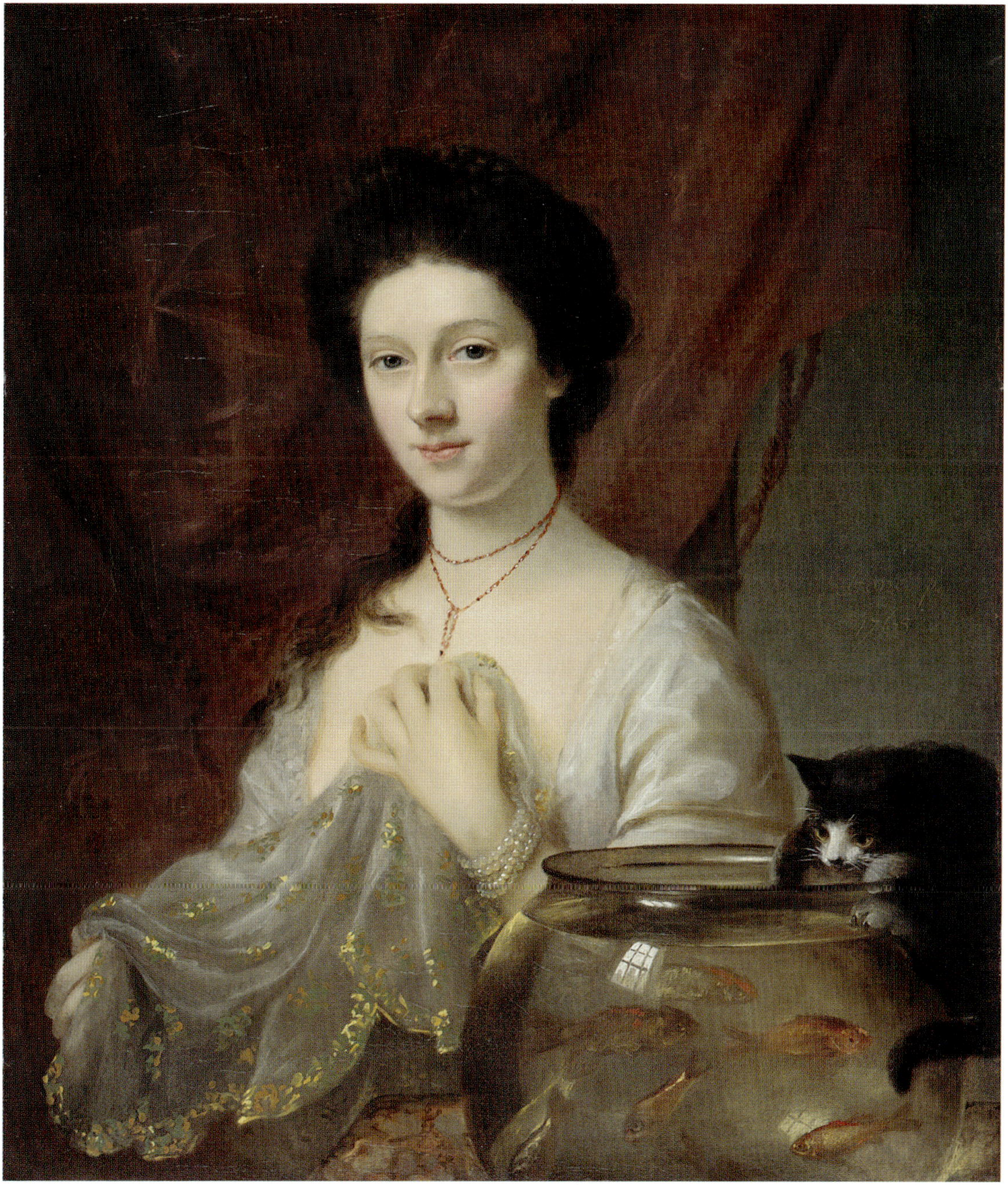

THE SHARP FAMILY

Johann Joseph Zoffany, 1779–81

This tour de force of a conversation piece was painted for William Sharp, the man at the back of the barge waving his hat, who was surgeon to George III. It depicts one of the regular family concerts given by this musical family, which in the summer were held in a barge on the Thames (Fulham Old Church can be seen in the background), and it remains one of the most vivid pictures of eighteenth-century family life. William's wife sits in front of him holding their 2-year-old daughter Mary, who, being too young to participate, has in the best traditions of eighteenth-century child portraiture been given a kitten to hold. Sharp's brother Grenville, sitting behind the spinet and French horns, was a well-known philanthropist and abolitionist. Their father, Thomas, in the bottom right-hand corner, was Archdeacon of Northumberland.

Zoffany, who was responsible for this feat of organisation and detail (there are eight musical instruments depicted), was born in Germany and, after a creditable start to his career painting late-baroque decorations and religious pieces, decided to try his fortune in England. He arrived in London in 1760 and by 1762 had been taken up by the great actor David Garrick, for whom he painted several family groups and more especially a number of scenes from Garrick's plays. Zoffany was in a sense able to pick up where Hogarth, who died in 1764, left off, and he took the conversation piece to new heights of sophistication. More coincidentally, like Hogarth with his pugs, he also introduced his own dog, a white German spitz called Poma, into his portraits. Sharp family tradition had it that the dog became so attached to them that it had to be included in the painting. Exactly the same rather tender view of the recumbent Poma, however, appeared again in Zoffany's portrait of John Wilkes and his daughter (fig. 8) of 1782. It seems likely that Zoffany was inclined to re-use

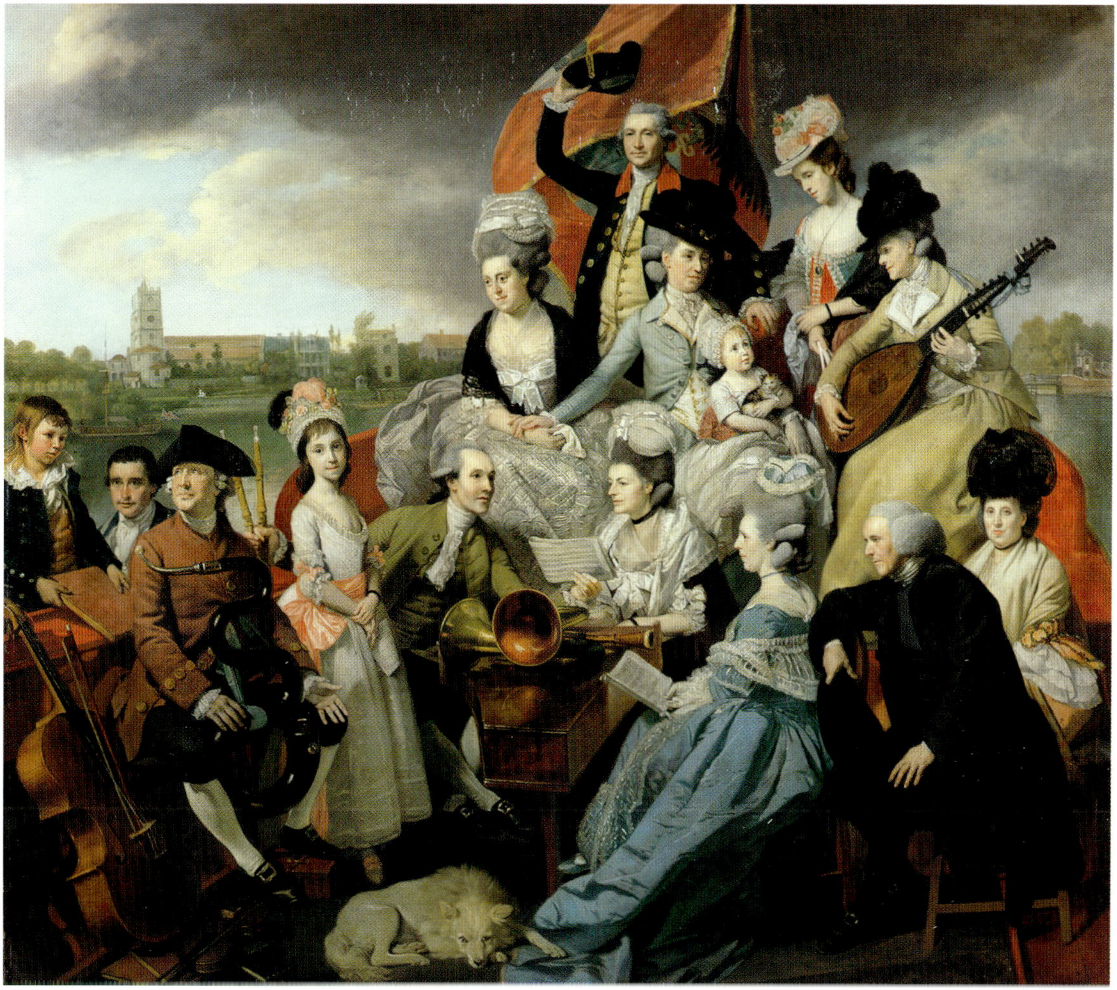

The Sharp Family by Johann Joseph Zoffany, 1779–81. Oil on canvas, 1156 x 1257mm. NPG L169. On loan to the National Portrait Gallery from the Trustees of the Lloyd-Baker Settled Estates

a good motif when he found one, especially if, as seems apparent with the Wilkeses, he found his sitters rather unsympathetic. A white spitz standing on its hind legs appears in at least two Zoffany conversation pieces from the late 1760s, though it seems more likely to be one of Poma's predecessors.

ROBERT BAKEWELL

John Boultbee, c.1788–90

Described rather quaintly in the *Oxford Dictionary of National Biography* as a grazier, Bakewell was in fact a pioneer of agricultural economics, and his stock-breeding programmes paved the way for today's specialised and intensive-farming techniques. He is portrayed here as the bachelor yeoman farmer that he was. Working from his country seat at Dishley Grange in Leicestershire, he experimented with his local Longhorn cattle to breed small-boned animals, producing the maximum amount of meat and fat in the shortest time to feed, and provide tallow candles for, the rapidly growing and industrialised population. The results of this programme were the ridiculously small-headed and cylindrical-bodied cattle familiar to us from early nineteenth-century paintings. Some of Bakewell's Longhorn cattle can be seen grazing in the field behind.

The artist John Boultbee was also a Leicestershire man, whose paintings at their best can be mistaken for those by Stubbs. He was quickly adopted by Bakewell to portray (and thus advertise through subsequent prints) his latest prize cattle. This portrait seems actually to have been commissioned by an associate of Bakewell's, John Fowler, and exists in four versions. That Boultbee was no Stubbs can be seen not only in the portrait's charming naivety but also in his problems with the horse's anatomy. Changes to the position of the horse's legs are visible in at least three of the different versions. This version is apparently the only one to show the little dog, which is probably some sort of local terrier. Gazing slightly reproachfully at its master, as if asking to be given a lift instead of having to run round after the horse, it adds a humane and narrative touch to the portrait of a man who, despite his calling and his grisly museum of pickled joints and skeletons, was known for his concern for his animals' welfare.

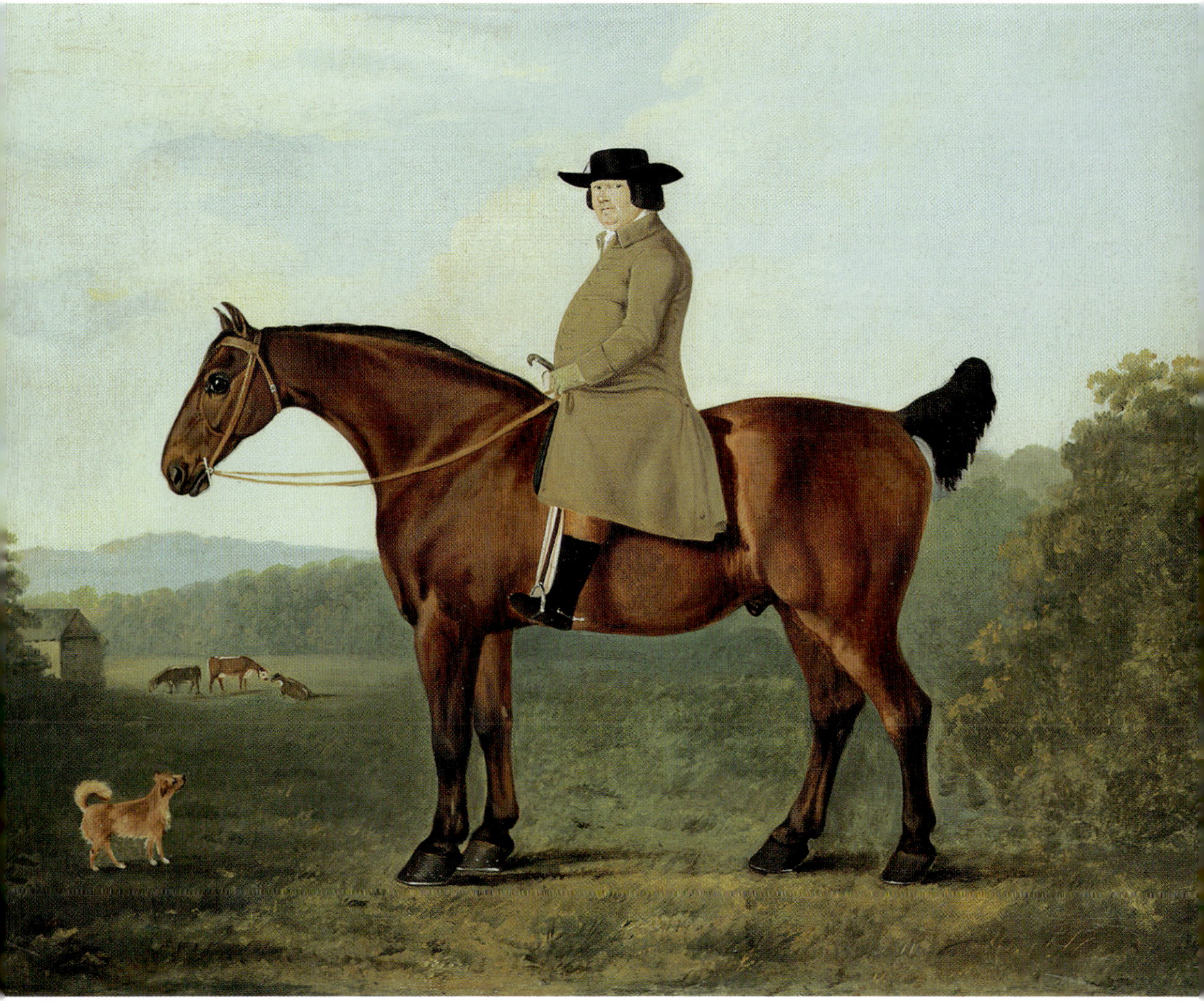

Robert Bakewell (1725–95) by John Boultbee, c.1788–90.
Oil on canvas, 710 x 910mm. NPG 5949

THOMAS JENKINS WITH HIS NIECE ANNA MARIA

Angelica Kauffmann, 1790

Thomas Jenkins went to Rome in the early 1760s to study painting. Finding he could make a better living from dealing in the wealth of antiquities currently being excavated, he remained there for the rest of his life and added banking to his accomplishments. Despite an unsavoury reputation for manufacturing and improving upon some of his antiquities, and taking hefty commissions for the sale of visiting artists' work, Jenkins was genuinely helpful to a number of artists, obtaining access for them to copy works in private collections and acting as their agent. He had handled the Swiss-born artist Angelica Kauffmann's financial affairs since she had arrived to settle in Rome with her new husband in 1782. A genuinely international figure, she had attracted the notice of the great classical scholar and art historian Johann Joachim Winckelmann with her dainty neo-classical paintings in Rome twenty years earlier, before moving to England in 1766. There she became a protégée of Sir Joshua Reynolds, a founder member of the Royal Academy of Arts, London, and was employed by the Adam brothers to decorate rooms and ceilings.

Kauffmann was obviously content with Jenkins's services, for she gave him as a gift this portrait of himself with the niece who had recently arrived to live with him in Rome. In the *Memorandum* of her pictures, she scrupulously noted: 'For Mr. Thomas Jenkins, English ... the portrait of the above and of his niece Anna Maria, likewise the portrait of the pet dog.' Nothing else is known of the pet dog, though its specific inclusion in the

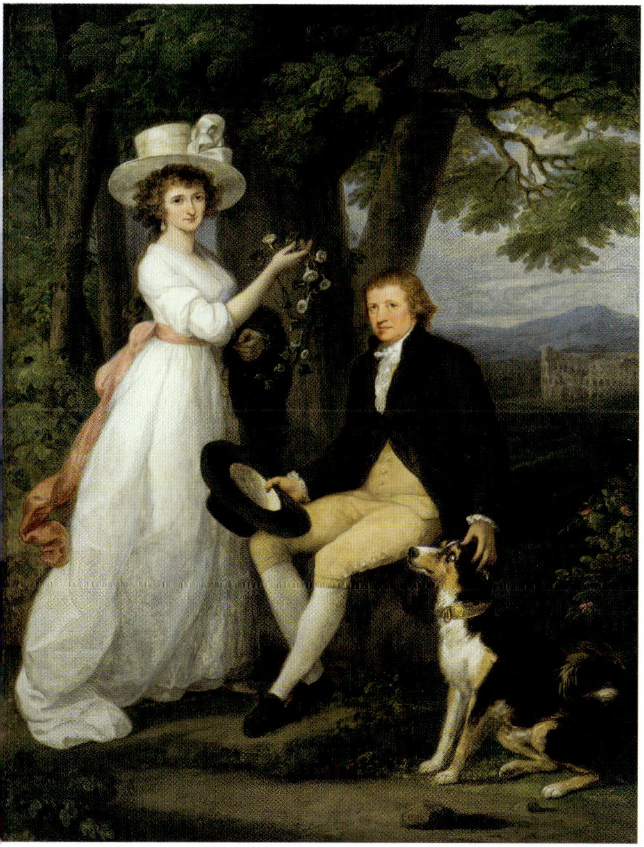

portrait, Jenkins's protective hand and the dog's look of adoration in return make it clear that this was a domestic rather than a sporting relationship. It looks a bit like a collie, but since Jenkins had been in Rome for nearly thirty years it is more likely to have been some sort of native Italian sheepdog. In the sylvan background, Kauffmann has included a somewhat incongruous view of the Colosseum, little suspecting perhaps that it was from a reliable contact there that Jenkins obtained many of his fake antiquities.

Thomas Jenkins (1722–98) with his niece Anna Maria by Angelica Kauffmann, 1790. Oil on canvas, 1295 x 946mm. NPG 5044

SIR FRANCIS CHANTREY

Self-portrait, c.1800

Though destined to become one of the most famous sculptors of his age, Chantrey was the son of a tenant farmer near Sheffield and had a modest reputation as a painter there before coming to London in 1802. He did not entirely abandon painting until 1808, at about the time he married his cousin from Yorkshire. This drawing was sent to some London friends soon after his arrival and, apart from being ironically inscribed in ink 'Sketch from nature', is also inscribed in pencil '(a bachelor)'. An accompanying note explains that the drawing was sent to say that he could not visit friends as usual since he was confined to his lodgings with mumps. Beneath the row of medicine bottles on the mantelpiece is the name of his doctor, Mr Merreyman.

While the attendant dogs and mother cat and kitten obviously serve to add poignancy to Chantrey's current predicament (and may of course have belonged to his landlady), Chantrey is known to have been very fond of animals. A pointer called Hector is recorded – though probably of later vintage than the small supplicant hound in the drawing – and, immortalised in paint, the Dandie Dinmont terrier called Mustard that was given to Chantrey by Sir Walter Scott in 1825 in return for his bust of the famous novelist. Scott had of course more or less invented Dandie Dinmonts in his novel *Guy Mannering; or The Astrologer* (1815), and in 1836 Chantrey commissioned from his friend Sir Edwin Landseer a portrait of Mustard sitting by a copy of the bust in a corner of his studio and keeping one of the sculptor's cats under the table at bay. Mustard had by then, alas, wrote Chantrey's biographer George Jones, 'increased his bulk, and he became a striking example of the effects of luxury and repletion, yet his obesity and indolence did not diminish his devotion to his master'.

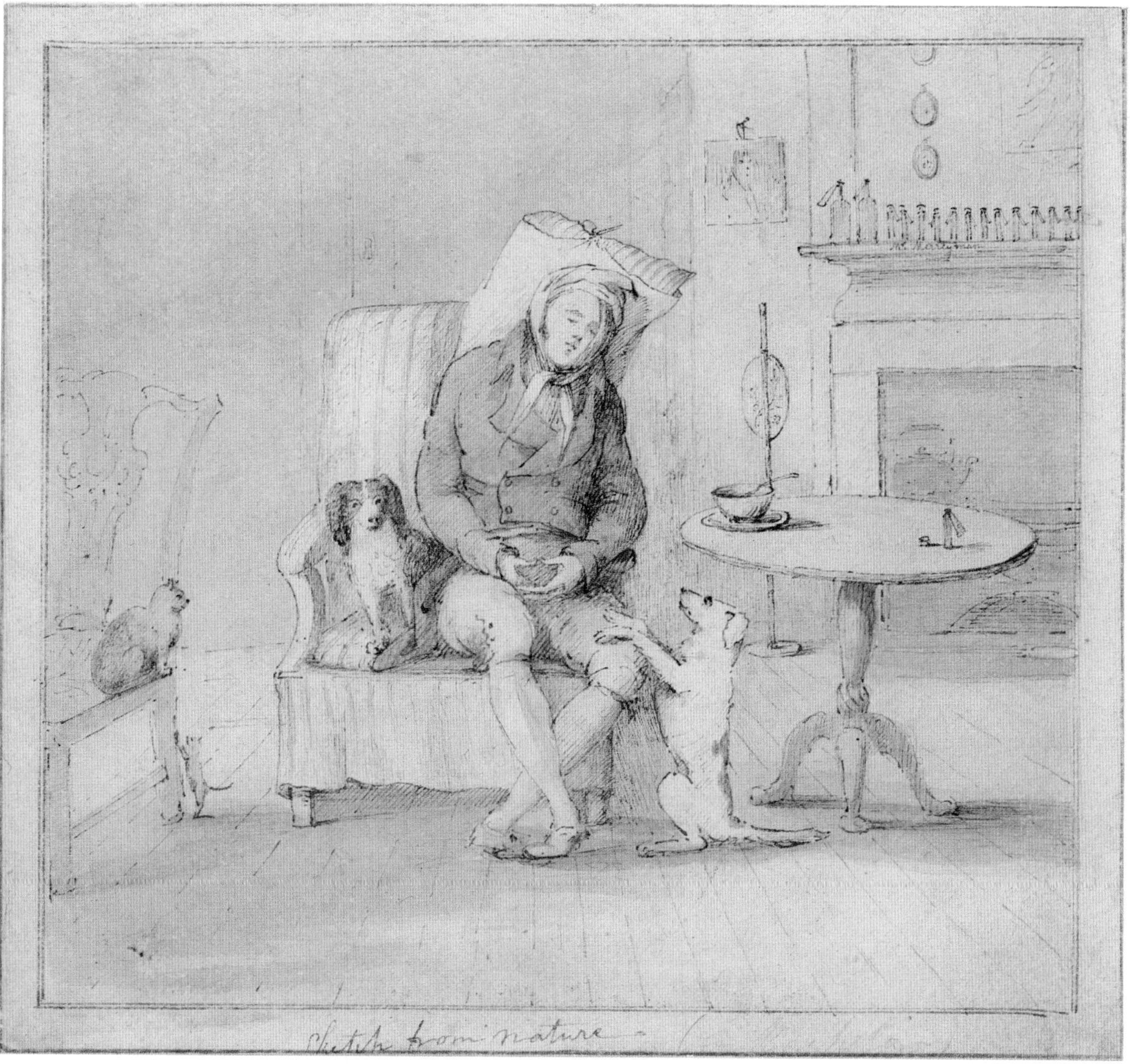

Sir Francis Leggatt Chantrey (1781–1841), self-portrait, c.1800. Pencil and grey wash, 136 x 143mm. NPG 2103a

LADY CAROLINE LAMB

Eliza H. Trotter, c.1810

Lady Caroline Lamb's famous note in her diary in 1812 after meeting Byron for the first time – 'mad, bad and dangerous to know' – was not only perspicacious but might equally well have been applied to herself. Married to William Lamb, the future Lord Melbourne and Prime Minister to Queen Victoria, she nevertheless became Byron's lover for several months before, finding her too much to handle, he terminated the relationship. She pursued him obsessively, becoming increasingly eccentric and even violent, especially so after the poet's death in 1824, when her long-suffering husband finally decided they must separate. She had written several highly romantic novels and some conventional verse, and after further romantic entanglements with younger men, such as the novelist Edward Bulwer-Lytton, died in London at the age of forty-two.

The circumstances of this rather amateurish but charming portrait by Eliza H. Trotter, the daughter of an Irish portrait painter, are not recorded, but the fact that it belonged to Caroline and the presence of the miniature bull terrier give a strong clue to its extraordinary origins in the scandalous world of Regency society. Dressed in the provocative 'see-through' neo-classical dress of the time, Caroline had allowed the portrait to be exhibited simply as *Portrait of a Young Lady* at the Royal Academy in 1811. To anyone who knew her well, its identity would of course have been obvious, and, like a later well-known portrait of her as a page by Thomas Phillips, it seems to have carried a coded message for those who could read it. The previous year, Caroline had begun her first extra-marital affair with a certain Sir

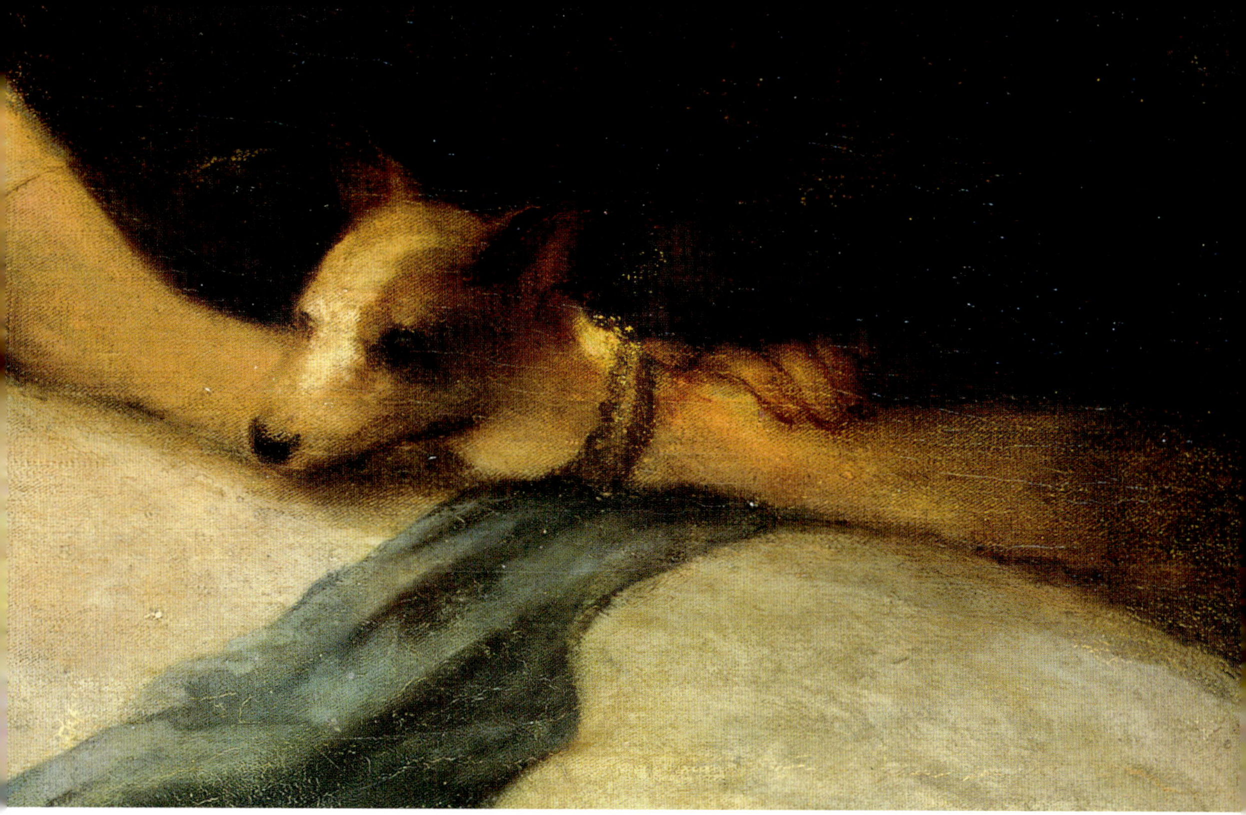

Godfrey Webster, who is recorded as giving her two presents, a bracelet and a dog. Both presents appear to be shown in this painting: the little dog can be seen wearing not only its own collar but also an apparently valuable bracelet – presumably Sir Godfrey's – of set-and-linked gemstones with a clasp.

This parading in public of a scandalous affair must have been extremely distressing to her family, and the portrait may well have been one of the factors that caused Lady Melbourne, her mother in law, to write to her: 'Had you been sincere in your promises of amendment, or wished to make any return to William [her husband] for his kindness, you would have discarded and driven from your presence any persons or thing which could remind you of the unworthy

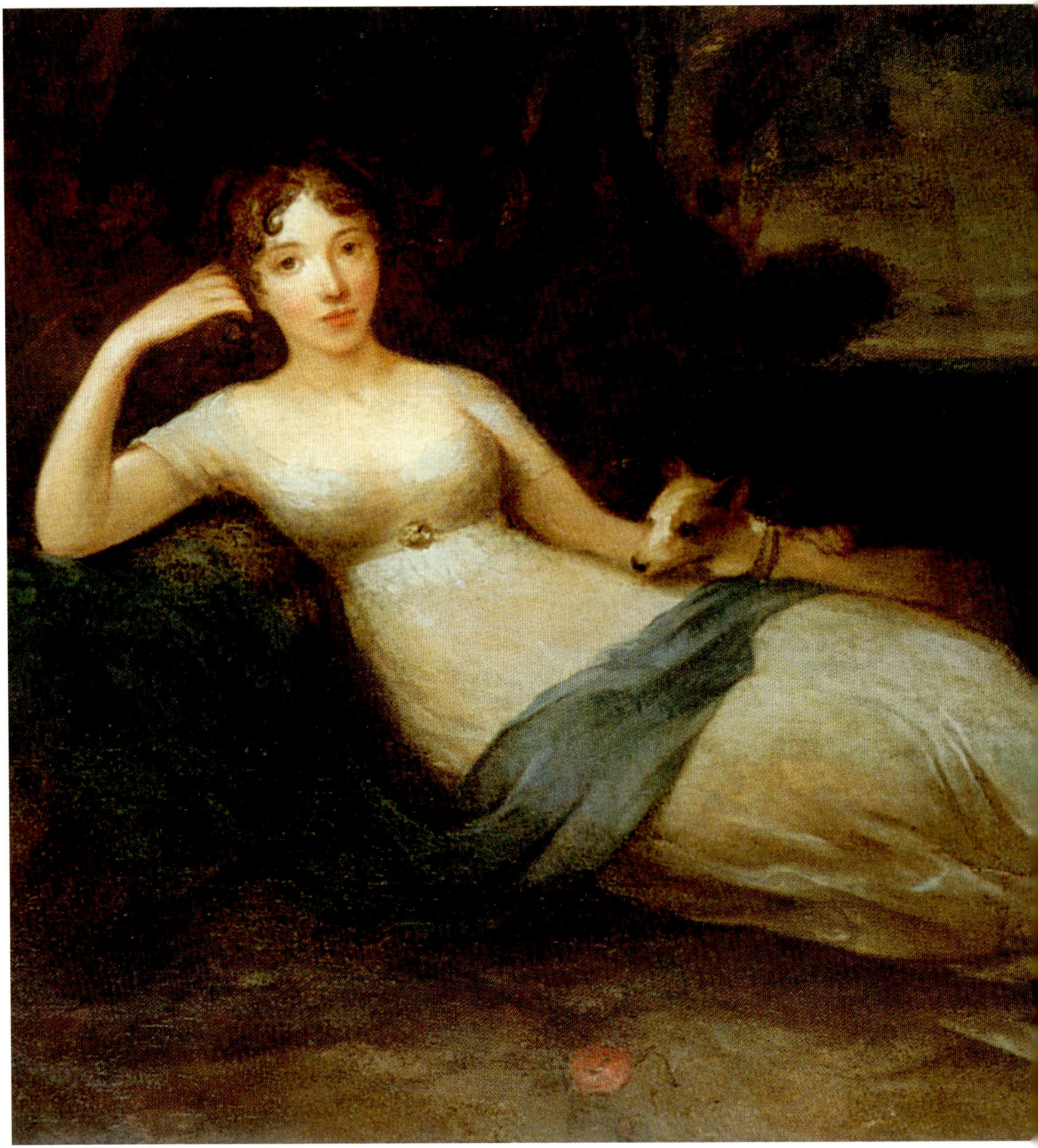

object [her lover] for whose sake you had run such risks and exposed yourself so much. But on the contrary you seem to delight in everything that recalls him to you.' In fact, the dog, whose name seems to have been Phyllis, eventually caused Caroline to repent after it had bitten her only son, Augustus. No reprisals against Phyllis appear to have been taken, however, and Caroline was soon writing to her husband from Brocket Hall, their country house: 'Plunger [her husband's dog?] ran away from me yesterday, and Francis found him parading at the top of the park with some stray poultry. I would not bring my pretty Phyllis, as you wished not.' If Phyllis were indeed Sir Godfrey's gift to his wife, one can appreciate Lamb's reluctance to be reminded of the fact. He may well have recalled an entry he made in his commonplace book in 1809: 'Before I was married, whenever I saw the children and the dogs allowed ... to be troublesome in a family, I used to lay it all to the fault of the master of it, who might at once put a stop to it if he pleased. Since I have married, I find that this was a very rash and premature judgement.'

Lady Caroline Lamb (1785–1828) by Eliza H. Trotter, c.1810 (exhibited 1811). Oil on canvas, 1149 x 1403mm. NPG 3312

SIR FRANCIS BURDETT

Sir William Ross, c.1840

This charming oversize miniature of an elderly country gentleman, dressed for riding and sitting in his library with his dog, contains perhaps only one clue to the fact that he was one of the most radical and outspoken politicians of his time: the bust, dominating the room, of his mentor, the famous political agitator of a previous generation, John Horne Tooke. A fearless advocate of free speech and the reform of the House of Commons, Burdett was a constant thorn in the side of the government and was twice imprisoned. By the time of this portrait, and with reform achieved, he was siding with the Tories, had more or less retired from active politics and was devoted to fox hunting.

Pursuing his humanitarian interests, Burdett was one of the sponsors of the Martin Act 1822, the first piece of legislation for protecting animals. He had married into the Coutts banking family, and his love of animals was amply inherited by his daughter, Baroness Angela Burdett-Coutts, the philanthropist and famous heiress to the banking fortune. She instituted countless schemes for improvements both in animal welfare and farming, became President of the RSPCA and erected the statue to the legendary Skye terrier Greyfriars Bobby in Edinburgh in 1872. She kept numerous pets at her house in Highgate, including llamas on the front lawn, a famous cockatoo called Cocky and her favourite dog, a small Manchester terrier called Fan, whose biography she wrote.

Her father's dog is less well documented and being, unusually, seen from behind is less easy to identify. It certainly seems a suitable companion for hunting, possibly an early form of Airedale terrier, and is well provided for by the unique and elegant water bowl, prophetic perhaps of the numerous drinking fountains for men and animals alike that his daughter would erect around the country.

Sir Francis Burdett, 5th Bt (1770–1844) by Sir William Ross, c.1840. Watercolour on ivory (miniature), 394 x 343mm. NPG 2056

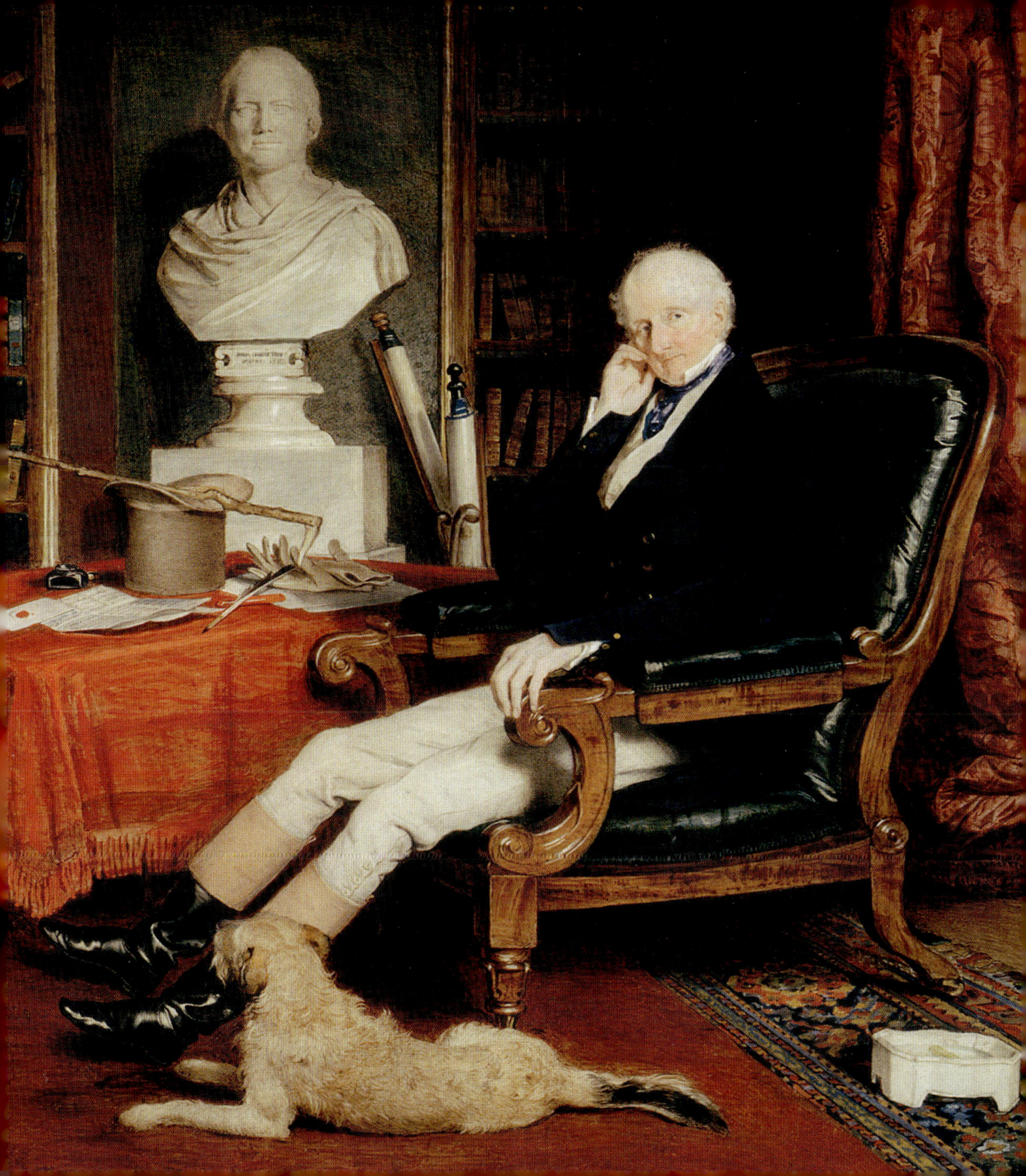

SIR EDWIN LANDSEER

John Ballantyne, c.1865

The most famous British artist of his day and certainly the greatest animal painter of the nineteenth century, Landseer was more or less obliged against his better judgement to undertake the monumental task of modelling the lions for the base of Nelson's Column in Trafalgar Square. He was occupied with the project on and off from 1858 to 1866, and there is little doubt that it was a major contributory factor to the ill health that clouded the last ten years of his life. After a barrage of sniping in the press about the commission being given to a painter and the lack of progress, he opened his studio in 1863 to a select gathering to view the initial 6-foot model, on which he had been working. Ballantyne's painting, one of a series of six famous artists in their studios, was probably based on

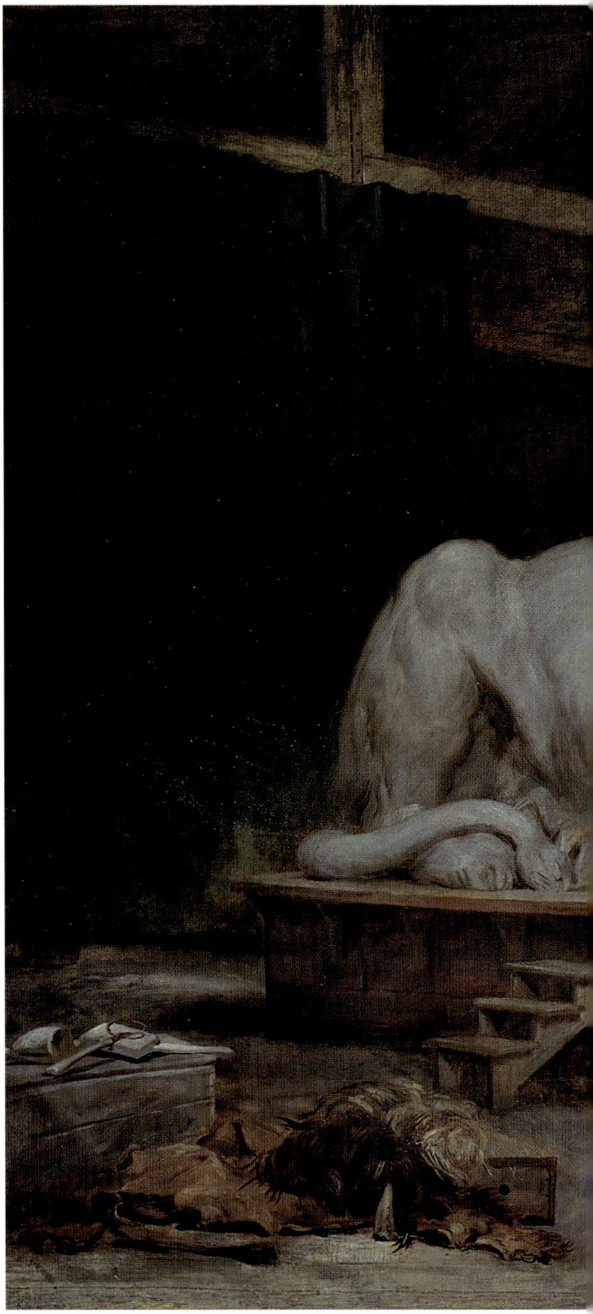

Sir Edwin Landseer (1802–73) by John Ballantyne, c.1865. Oil on canvas, 800 x 1130mm. NPG 835

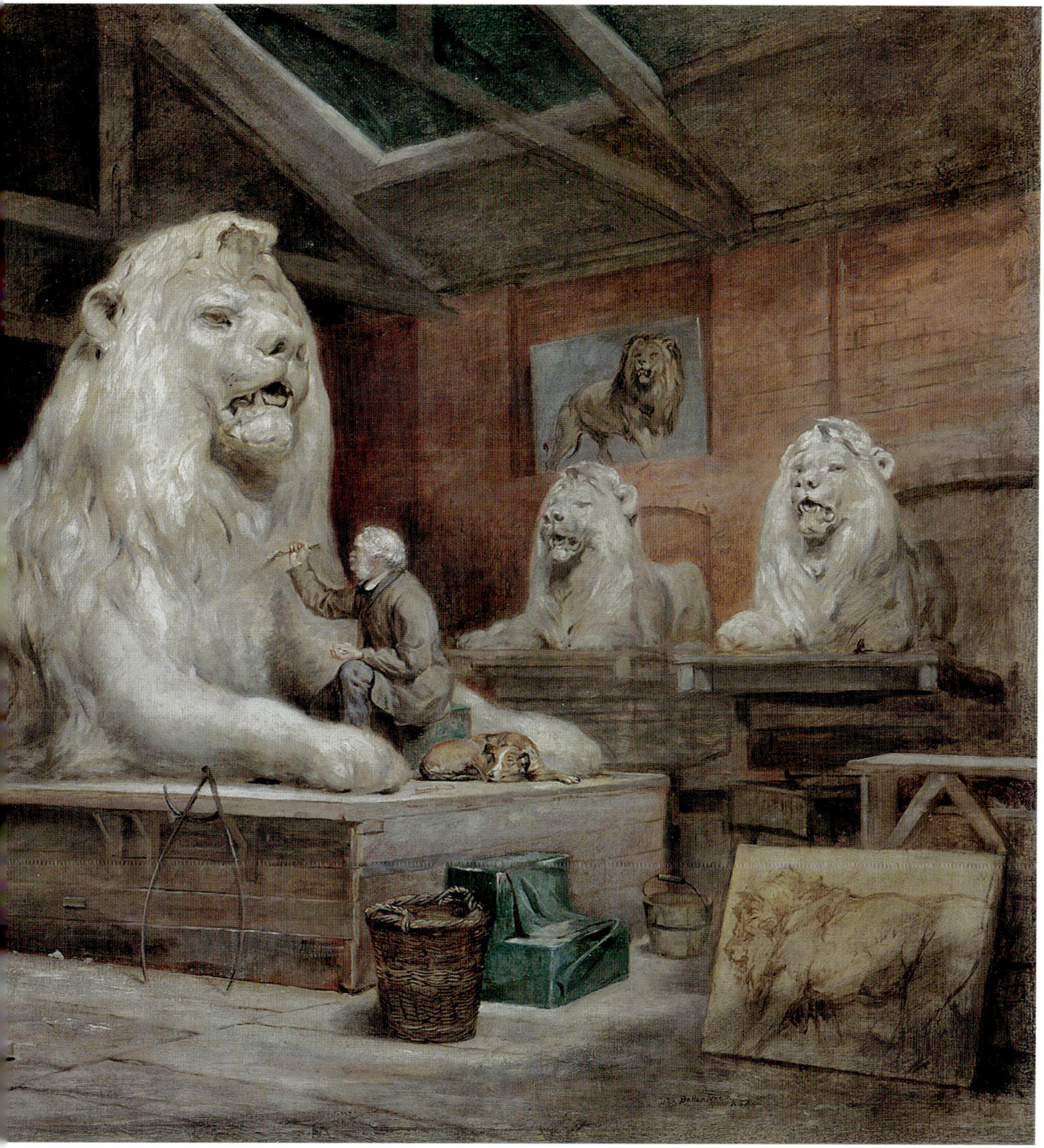

photographs taken around this time. It shows Landseer at work on the final 20-foot model in the borrowed studio of the sculptor Baron Carlo Marochetti, who was eventually responsible for casting the four bronzes, which were finally put in place in January 1867.

Landseer owned a number of dogs all his life, and acute observation of his own pets – combined with a strong vein of sentiment and an immaculate technique – undoubtedly helped to make him the greatest and most successful painter of dogs of all time. As such, he was one of the very small number of artists whose work appealed to Queen Victoria, and she and Prince Albert commissioned a large number of paintings of their own extensive collection of dogs. The brown dog on the platform here, patiently attending her master, is almost certainly Landseer's faithful collie Lassie, who was known to have been his constant companion in the studio at this time. Her appearance agrees well with the one in a famous self-portrait, also of 1865, called *The Connoisseurs*, which Landseer later presented to Edward, Prince of Wales.

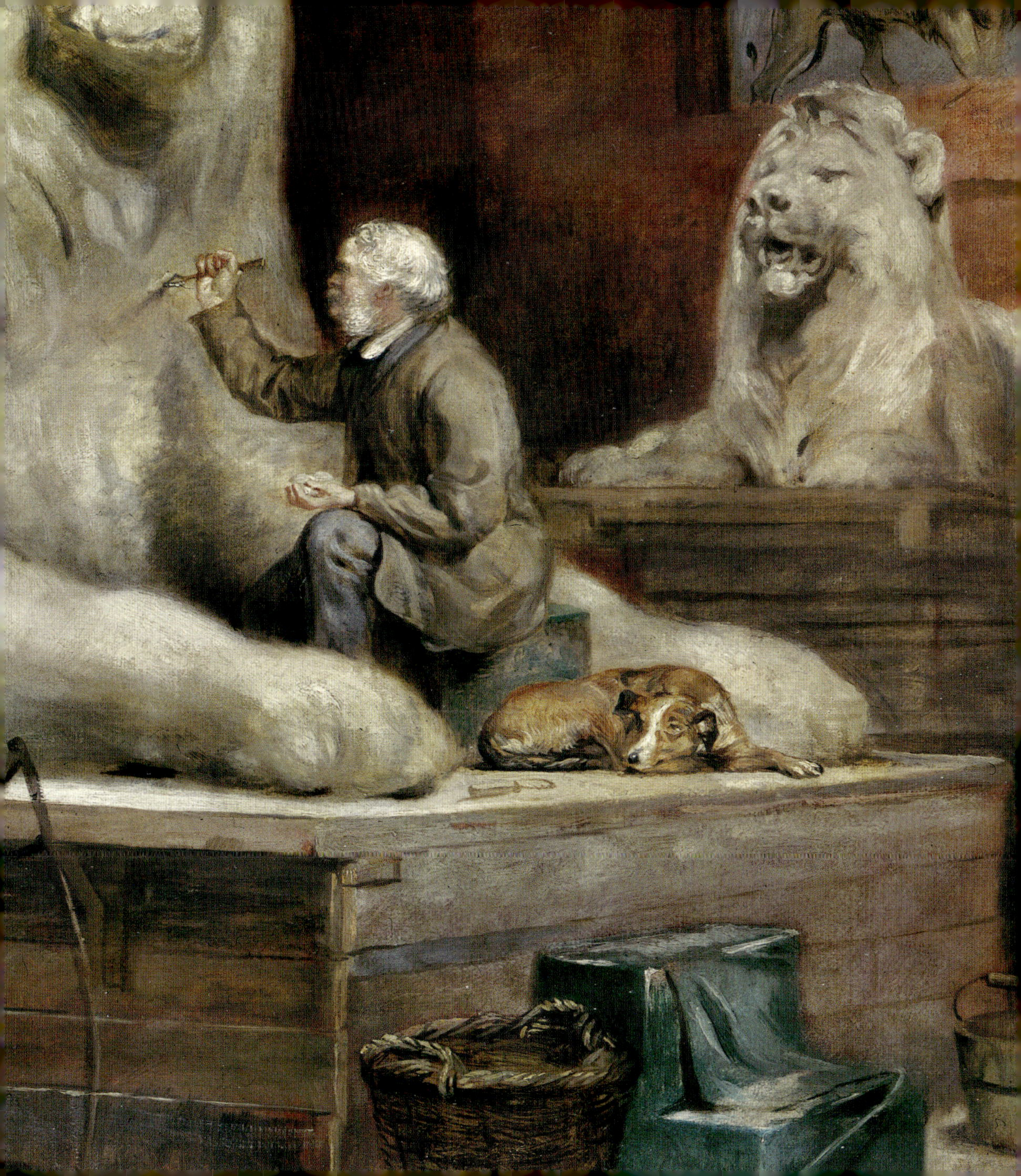

CHARLES READE

Attributed to Charles Mercier, c.1870

Author of *The Cloister and the Hearth* (1861) and *It Is Never too Late to Mend* (1856), Reade was one of the most popular of all Victorian novelists and dramatists, though his work has not stood the test of time. With an inclination for melodrama, he was a sort of English Victor Hugo, though his social concerns led him to associate himself with Emile Zola, whose *L'Assommoir* he adapted for the stage under the uncompromising title of *Drink* (1879). Given the striking respectability of this most Victorian of interiors, his private life has long been the subject of speculation, and for nearly thirty years he lived with an actress, then described as his housekeeper and hostess, Mrs Laura Seymour.

Relatives recalled that the room depicted in this portrait was in his house at 2 Albert Terrace, Knightsbridge, London, and that 'in a large room on the ground floor, looking into Hyde Park, which he called his workshop, he laboured until the end of his life for at least one hour every afternoon at ponderous ledgers, which he filled with notes or cuttings from books or newspapers on topics that appealed to his interest.' There is little doubt that the painting depicts one of these afternoons, and his cat with her two kittens doze lazily on one of the many ledgers scattered round the room. Reade was said to have had a whole menagerie, but his niece remembered the white German spitz waiting patiently to be taken out into the park belonged to Mrs Seymour and was called Puff. One of the portraits on the walls, presumably the one on the right, was of Mrs Seymour. Reade never recovered from her death in 1879 and was buried beside her in Willesden five years later.

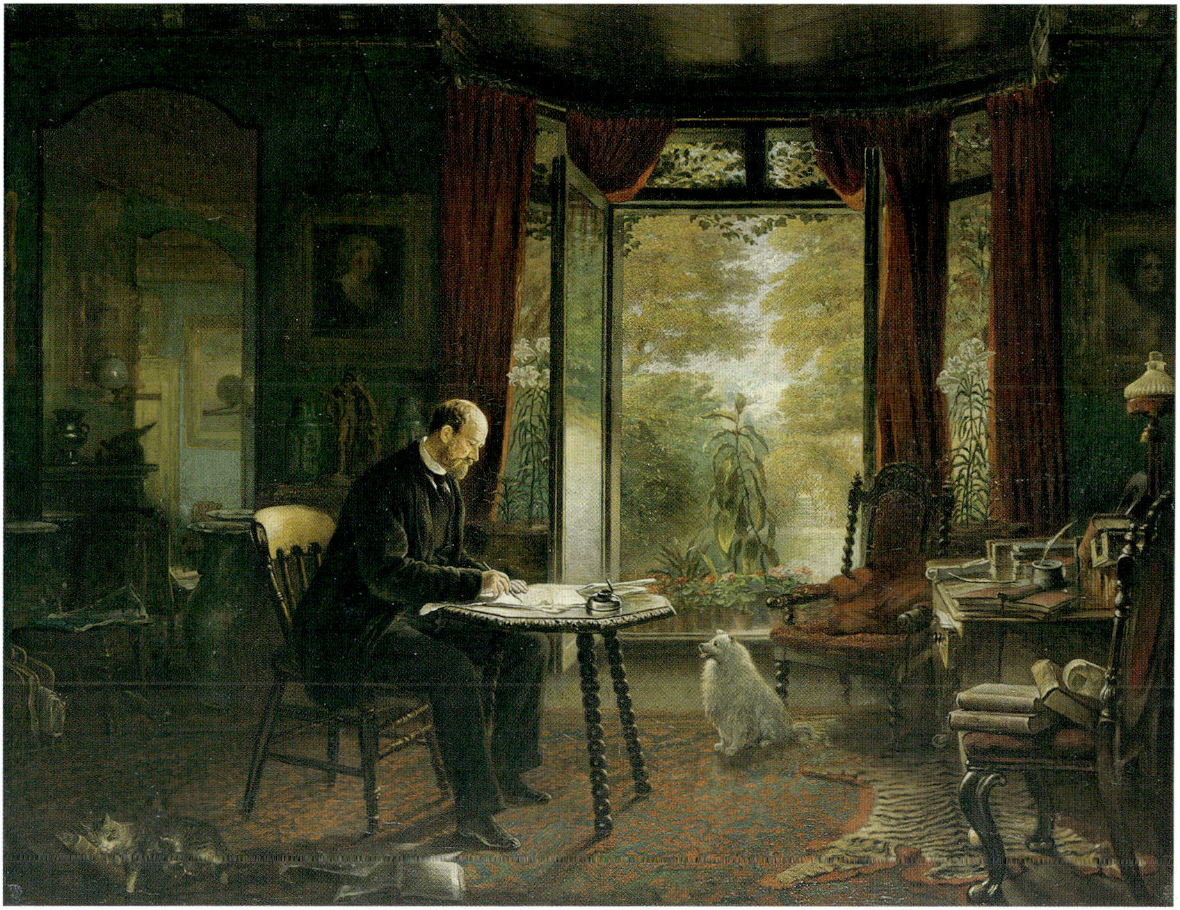

Charles Reade (1814–84) attributed to Charles Mercier, c.1870. Oil on canvas, 1099 x 1403mm. NPG 2281

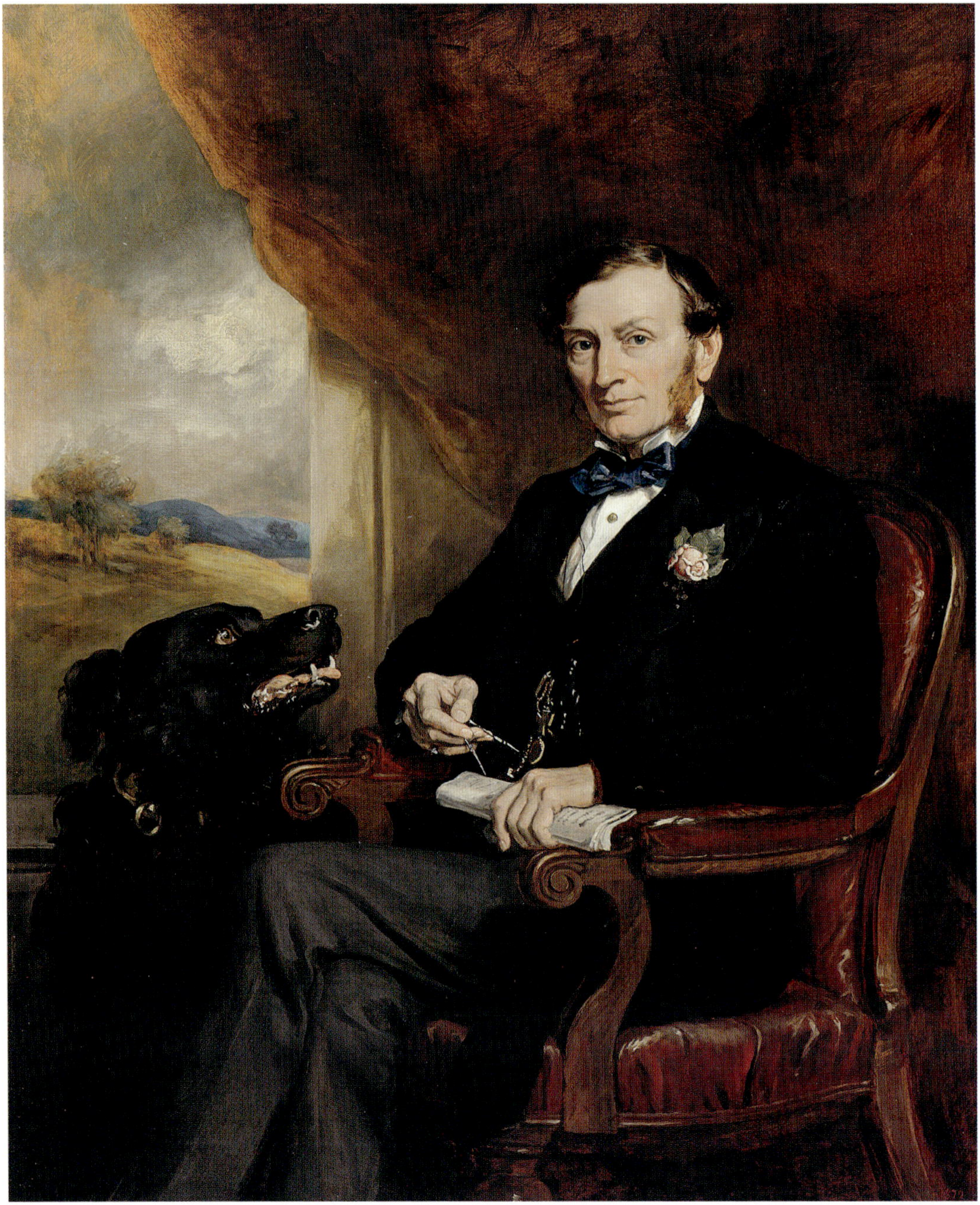

SIR DANIEL GOOCH

Sir Francis Grant, 1872

As a boy in Northumberland, Gooch had sat on George Stephenson's knee and acquired a lifelong love of steam engines. In 1837, at the age of twenty-one, he was appointed locomotive superintendent of the Great Western Railway and worked with his friend Isambard Kingdom Brunel on designing and improving locomotives for Brunel's broad-gauge track and laying the foundations for the modern railway system. He received his baronetcy in 1866 for inaugurating the Trans-Atlantic Telegraph and had sent and received the first cable messages to America earlier that year. Returning to the Great Western in 1865, he rescued it from bankruptcy and was subsequently instrumental in the construction of the Severn and Mersey tunnels. The only clue to all these achievements in Sir Francis Grant's urbane portrait is the pair of dividers that Gooch holds in his hand. Instead, he shows him as the country gentleman and MP that he had become, sitting in bourgeois splendour next to a view suggestive of his native Northumberland moors, with his large black retriever by his side.

Before he became a painter, Grant had not only studied for the law but was also a keen fox-hunting enthusiast. He painted one of the last portraits of Sir Walter Scott, showing the novelist with his deerhounds, in 1831 (Scottish National Portrait Gallery, Edinburgh) and much of his mature work is of hunting groups or equestrian portraits. As such he enjoyed a friendly rivalry with Sir Edwin Landseer and became President of the Royal Academy when Landseer declined the post in 1866. Grant's painting of Gooch's panting black retriever is a tour de force not unworthy of Landseer, though totally without the latter's sentimentality. Retrievers were a relatively new group, originally developed in Britain specifically as gun dogs from crossings principally between Newfoundlands and Labradors, though this long-haired black variety does not correspond to any of today's breed standards. It may have been a forerunner of the flat-coated retriever.

Sir Daniel Gooch, 1st Bt (1816–89) by Sir Francis Grant, 1872. Oil on canvas, 1422 x 1118mm. NPG 5080

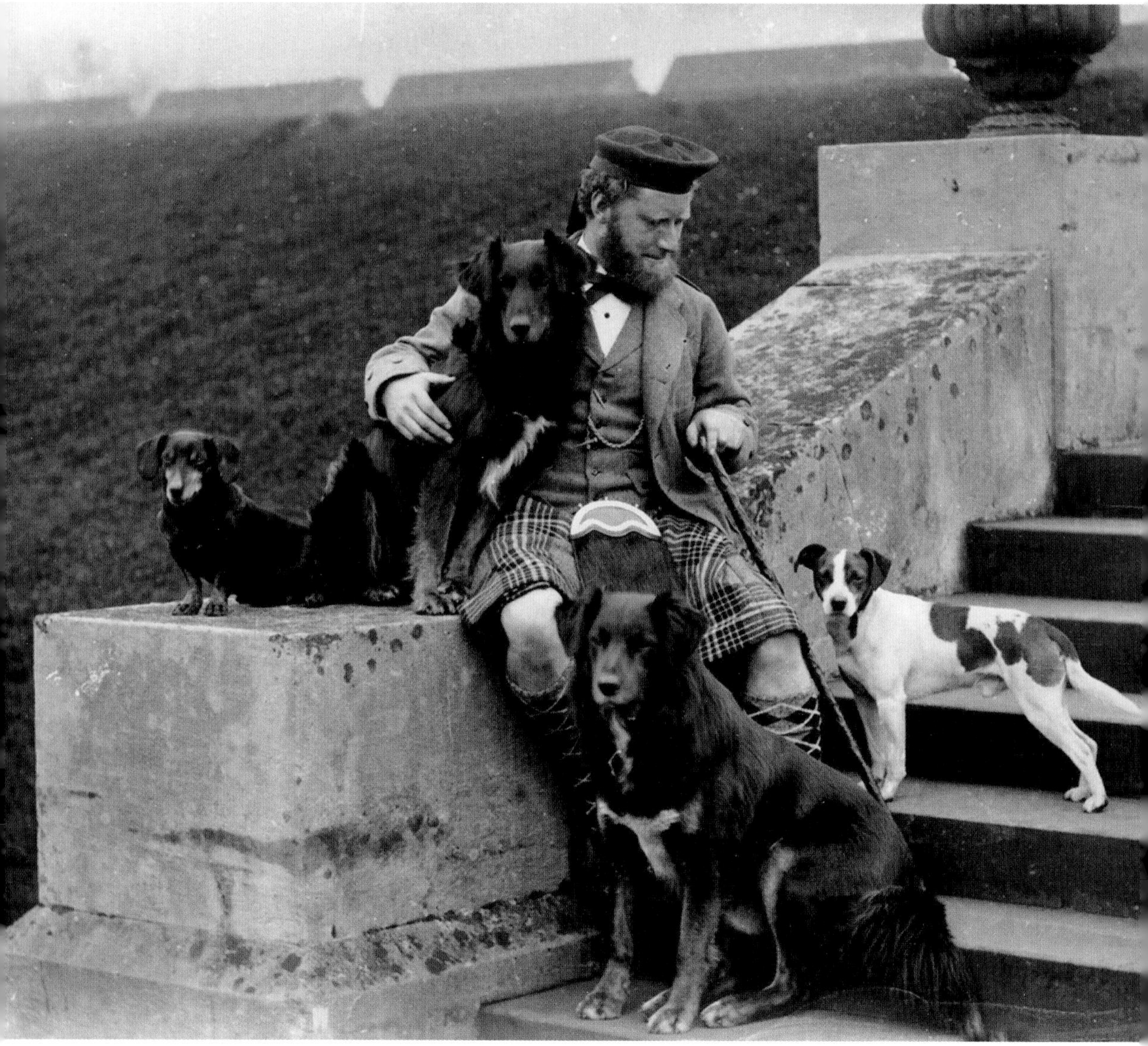

John Brown (1826–83) by Hills & Saunders, early 1880s.
Modern print from half-plate glass negative. NPG x35278

JOHN BROWN

Hills & Saunders, early 1880s

Appointed by Prince Albert in 1849, John Brown became Queen Victoria's gillie and personal servant in Scotland, but by 1864 he had been brought south to Osborne and before long had become totally indispensable to her. Hated by most of the Royal Family and despised by the court for his coarseness and rudeness, his privileged position was not without its stresses, and he took to heavy drinking. Despite looking hale and hearty in this photograph, he died prematurely a few years later.

This photograph appears to have been taken below the south terrace at Windsor and shows Brown entrusted with the Queen's favourite dogs of the period. The smooth fox terrier, whom Brown seems at pains to keep under control with his stick, appears in a commemorative portrait by C. Burton Barber that Victoria had commissioned a few months after Brown's death and is identified as Wat. The border collie with the striking white T-mark on his chest, seated on the steps below, is one of a dynasty of at least four collies called Noble and also appears in the Barber painting. From other paintings by Barber in the Royal Collection, it is possible to conjecture with some certainty that the collie in Brown's embrace was called Fern. Equally, the little smooth-coated dachshund, Waldmann, was the second of Victoria's dachshunds of that name, many of them gifts from relatives in Germany. She had acquired him in Baden in 1872, and when he died in February 1881 she wrote in her diary: 'Such a dear kind little dog – & kept all the others in order.'

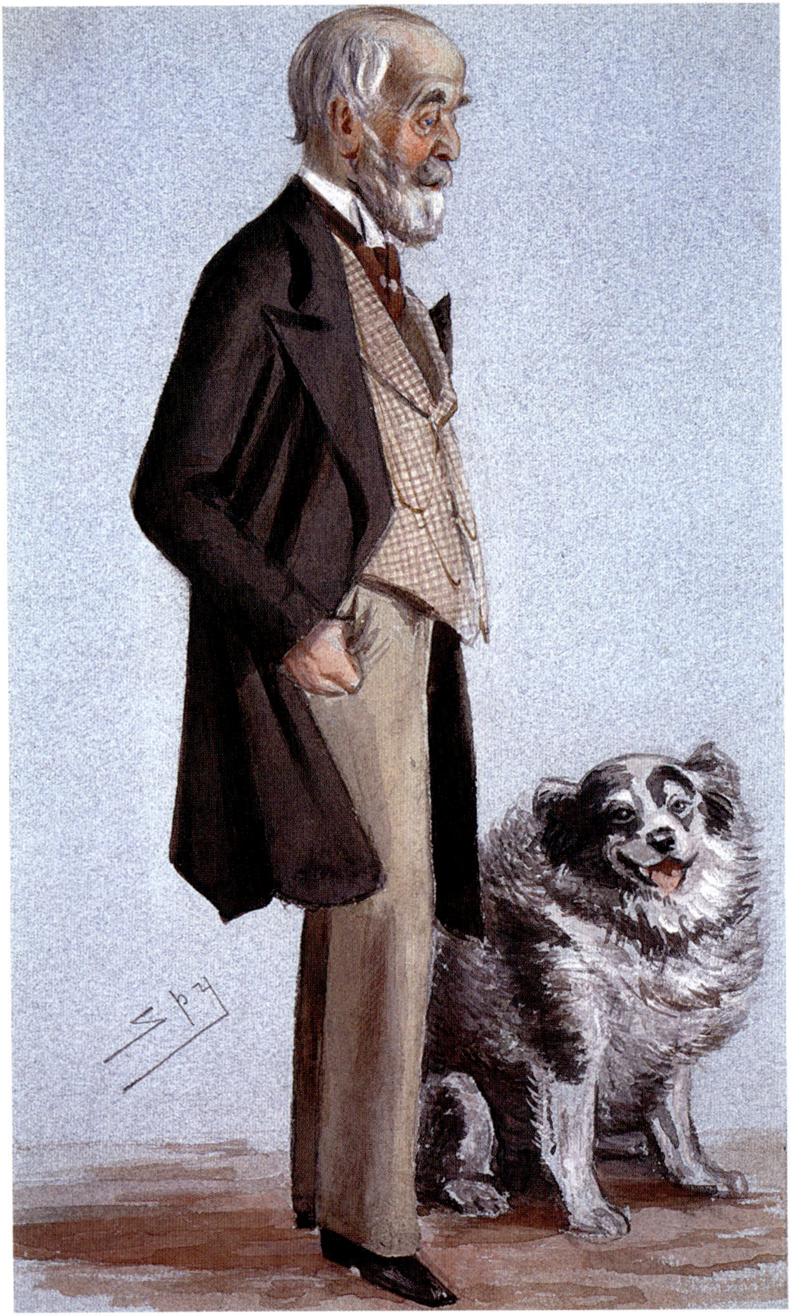

Alan, 3rd Baron Gardner (1810–83) by Sir Leslie Ward ('Spy'), 1883. Watercolour, 305 x 181mm. NPG 3287

ALAN, 3RD BARON GARDNER

Sir Leslie Ward ('Spy'), 1883

The title of this cartoon when published in the magazine *Vanity Fair* was 'Fox Hunting', rather surprisingly perhaps in view of the affable old gentleman depicted and his grossly overweight collie. Lord Gardner had in his younger days, however, been a member of the most fashionable circles, a friend of Count D'Orsay and Lady Blessington, and a legendary huntsman. Now, as *Vanity Fair* notes, he had become a good shot and taken up salmon fishing.

Working under the pseudonym 'Spy', Sir Leslie Ward produced many drawings that were, unlike most caricatures, done from actual sittings with his subjects, and the portraits of both master and dog here have an authentic feel to them. Lord Gardner died soon after the publication of this drawing, and one might speculate that the ageing collie was not long in following him. Collies had become very fashionable since receiving the royal seal of approval, and Queen Victoria owned a number of them in her widowhood. In the 1870s, her favourite collie, Sharp, had his portrait exhibited at the Royal Academy in London.

ELLEN TERRY

William Henry Grove, 1889

Writing in 1914 from Australia to her great friend, the painter, writer and dog owner W. Graham Robertson, on one of the punishing lecture tours she undertook in later life, the great actress remembered some of the many dogs she had known: 'I cd think of nothing but Dogs for a long while – they were much easier to think of than people – & I babbled of Snob – Winkie – Charley – Fussy [*sic*] – Drummy & Bossy as well of all my *later* ducks – (Dogs –).' Fussie was the fox terrier she had acquired from the famous jockey Fred Archer in the mid-1880s and, since he was the first fox terrier she had owned, may reasonably be assumed to be one of the two being tempted with titbits by his mistress, apparently on a stage set. The other is probably Drummy or Bossy.

It was in 1878 that Ellen Terry finally went into regular partnership with her great opposite number, Henry Irving, at the Lyceum Theatre and went on to create some of her most memorable roles. The relationship with Irving was a close though informal one, and she and Fussie accompanied Irving on all his American tours between 1883 and 1897. Gradually, however, as Ellen Terry remembered in her autobiography, Fussie 'had his affections alienated by a course of chops, tomatoes, strawberries, "ladies' fingers" soaked in champagne and a beautiful fur rug of his very own presented by Baroness Burdett-Coutts!', and his ownership was officially transferred to Irving.

As Irving's dog, Fussie's exploits and requirements became legendary. He had his own chair in Irving's dressing-room, made (unscheduled) appearances on stage round the world, found his way from Southampton back to the Lyceum

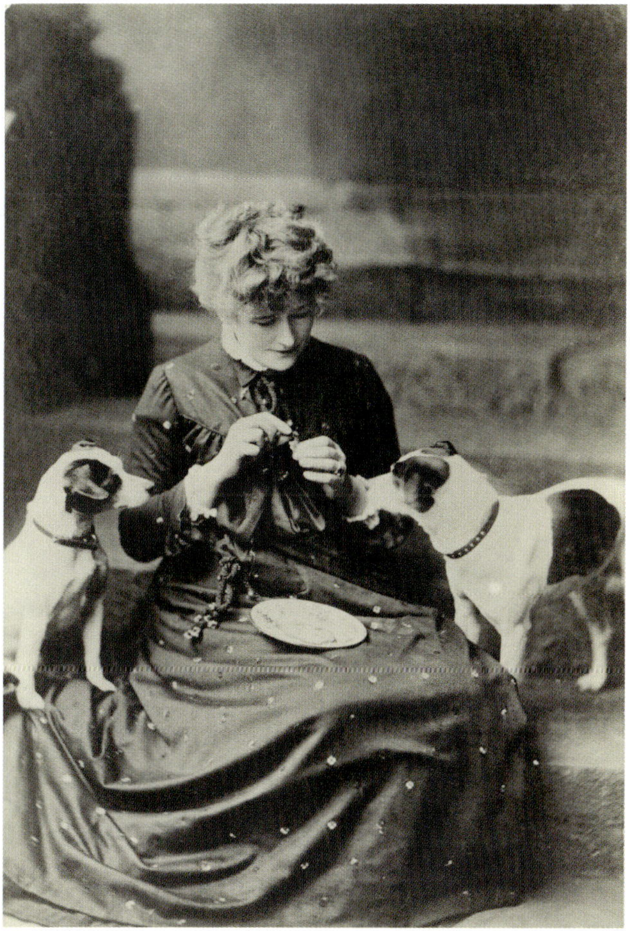

after missing the boat to America for the 1888 tour and, after missing the train from New York, was discovered by the station master trotting dutifully after it down the line to California. Fussie met his end in 1897 after falling through a trap door on the stage in Manchester. 'Henry was not told until the end of the play ... We drove [to the hotel] and found him there eating his supper with the poor dead Fussie, who would never eat supper any more, curled up in his rug on the sofa ... He is buried in the dogs' cemetery, Hyde Park.'

Ellen Terry (1847–1928) by an William Henry Grove, 1889. Bromide postcard print, 132 x 87mm. NPG x17049

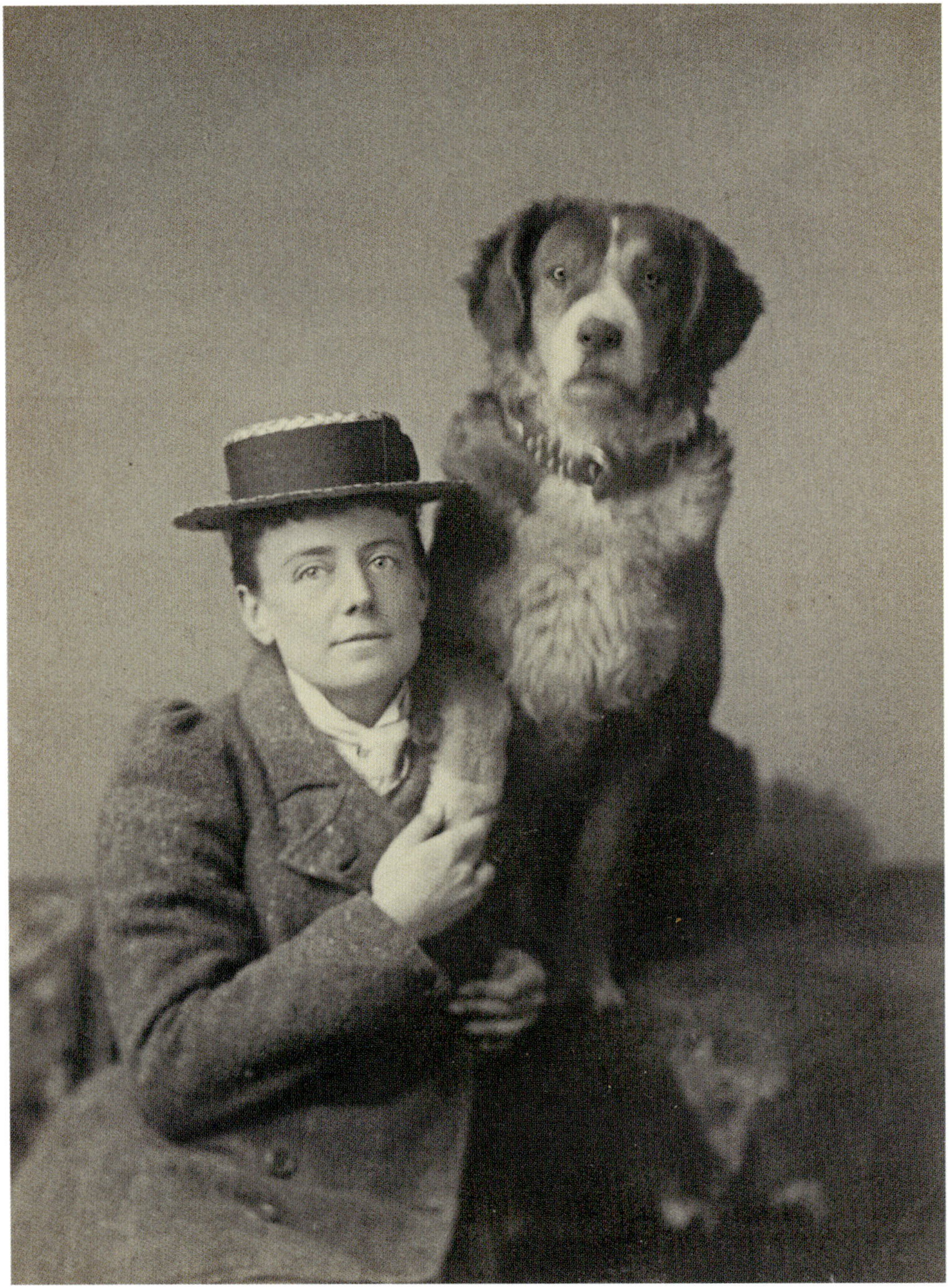

Dame Ethel Mary Smyth (1858–1944) with Marco by an unknown photographer, c.1891. Platinum print, 142 x 106mm. NPG x13395

DAME ETHEL SMYTH WITH MARCO

Unknown photographer, c.1891

As a pioneer campaigner for women's rights and the first British woman composer to achieve international renown, Dame Ethel's least-known work may well be *Inordinate (?) Affection*, an autobiographical account of her dogs that she published in 1936, just after the loss of Pan IV, one of a series of Old English sheepdogs, all called Pan.

'The incomparable Marco', as she calls him, was her first dog (pictured here). A St Bernard cross, he had been acquired by a friend from a Viennese washerwoman who had, like others of her trade, intended to use him to pull the little cart with which she collected the washing. As a student composer of songs and chamber music, Ethel had been living and studying in Leipzig since 1877 and, after the painful break-up of a passionate friendship with the wife of her first teacher in 1885, was clearly ready for a different sort of relationship. Indeed the succession of large dogs that dominated her later life seems to have played a part in fulfilling the emotional needs that her exuberant and friendly nature demanded.

The relationship with Marco, whom she took back to Leipzig in 1887, was clearly a marriage made in heaven. Before she finally returned to England with him in 1889, he had, as she relates with transparent relish, burst in on a rehearsal with Brahms and almost knocked him off the piano stool, demolished a hotel room during a trip to the Paris Exhibition and terrified Tchaikovsky, who nevertheless added a cautious PS to a letter of 11 April 1889: 'J'espère que votre *cher chien* va bien' ('I hope your *dear dog* is well'). Within a year her first orchestral music had been performed, and in 1893 the Mass in D, one of her most important works, was given its premiere. Professionally and emotionally she was out of what she later described as her 'desert'.

QUEEN ALEXANDRA

Sir Luke Fildes, 1894 (replica 1920)

The daughter of King Christian IX of Denmark, Alexandra married the Prince of Wales, the future Edward VII, in 1863 and made herself widely loved both for her charitable work and for her beauty. Her work for hospitals is still commemorated annually in Alexandra Rose day. When the National Portrait Gallery approached her son King George V in 1920 to enquire about the possibility of obtaining a portrait of her, he commissioned the artist Sir Luke Fildes to produce this replica of a portrait originally painted to commemorate his marriage to Princess Mary in 1894.

Although Alexandra had grown up with dogs in Denmark, it must have amazed her to see the huge number and range of dogs kept by her mother-in-law, Queen Victoria, in the royal kennels at Windsor. She continued the tradition with enthusiasm and, like Victoria, benefited from diplomatic gifts of the latest breeds from abroad. The first Pekinese, originally brought to Victoria in 1861, remained favourites all Alexandra's life. One called Little Billie slept at the foot of her bed and is said to have accompanied her to Russia. After the opening up of Japan to foreigners in the 1870s and 1880s, other breeds began to appear, including the Japanese Chin pictured here. Alexandra owned a number of these, though the date of the portrait and the dog's markings suggest that this is probably Punch, who was a special favourite and appears in several photographs with her. It is difficult to imagine that he was not also chosen to go with her dress.

Queen Alexandra (1844–1925) by Sir Luke Fildes, 1894 (replica 1920). Oil on canvas, 1283 x 1029mm. NPG 1889

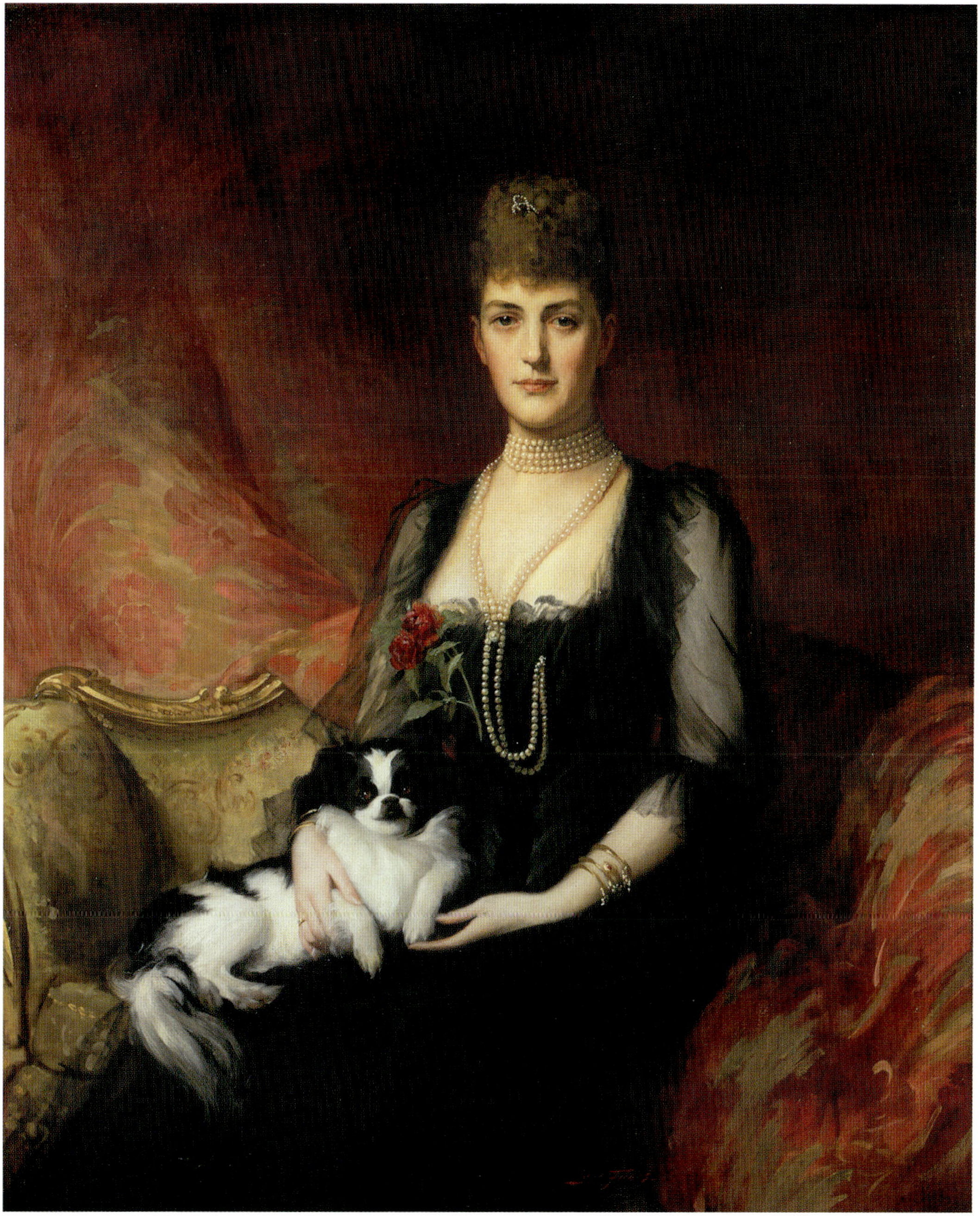

KING EDWARD VII

Thomas Heinrick Voigt, c.1910

Though better remembered for his beautiful Queen and for a number of famous mistresses, one of the most constant and faithful companions of Edward VII's last years seems to have been the small terrier called Caesar. As can be seen from the numerous retouchings around the dog, the photograph is in fact a fake, in which Caesar, who wore a collar inscribed 'I am Caesar, the King's dog', was reunited with his master and the result issued as a postcard by an enterprising German photographer after the King's death in 1910.

Caesar, described unconvincingly as a long-haired fox terrier (though one of his parents may have answered to that description), had been the King's constant companion in private life for seven years or so but shot to fame at the King's funeral when he was delegated by Queen Alexandra to follow the coffin in the procession from Westminster Hall on its way to Windsor. An already emotional nation was moved to tears at the sight of the somewhat disreputable-looking terrier trotting behind the gun-carriage, and entrepreneurs were quick to produce suitable souvenirs like this postcard. One quick-witted publisher even brought out a memoir entitled *Where's Master?*. According to Lord Esher, who went to tea at Buckingham Palace several weeks later, 'Caesar ... won't go near the Queen – and waits all day for his master, wandering about the house.' There was indeed little love lost between Caesar and the Queen, who preferred rather better-bred dogs. 'Horrid little dog,' she exclaimed to Margot Asquith, whose husband had told her that he had seen Caesar after the King's death lying at his feet: 'For warmth, my dear,' explained the Queen.

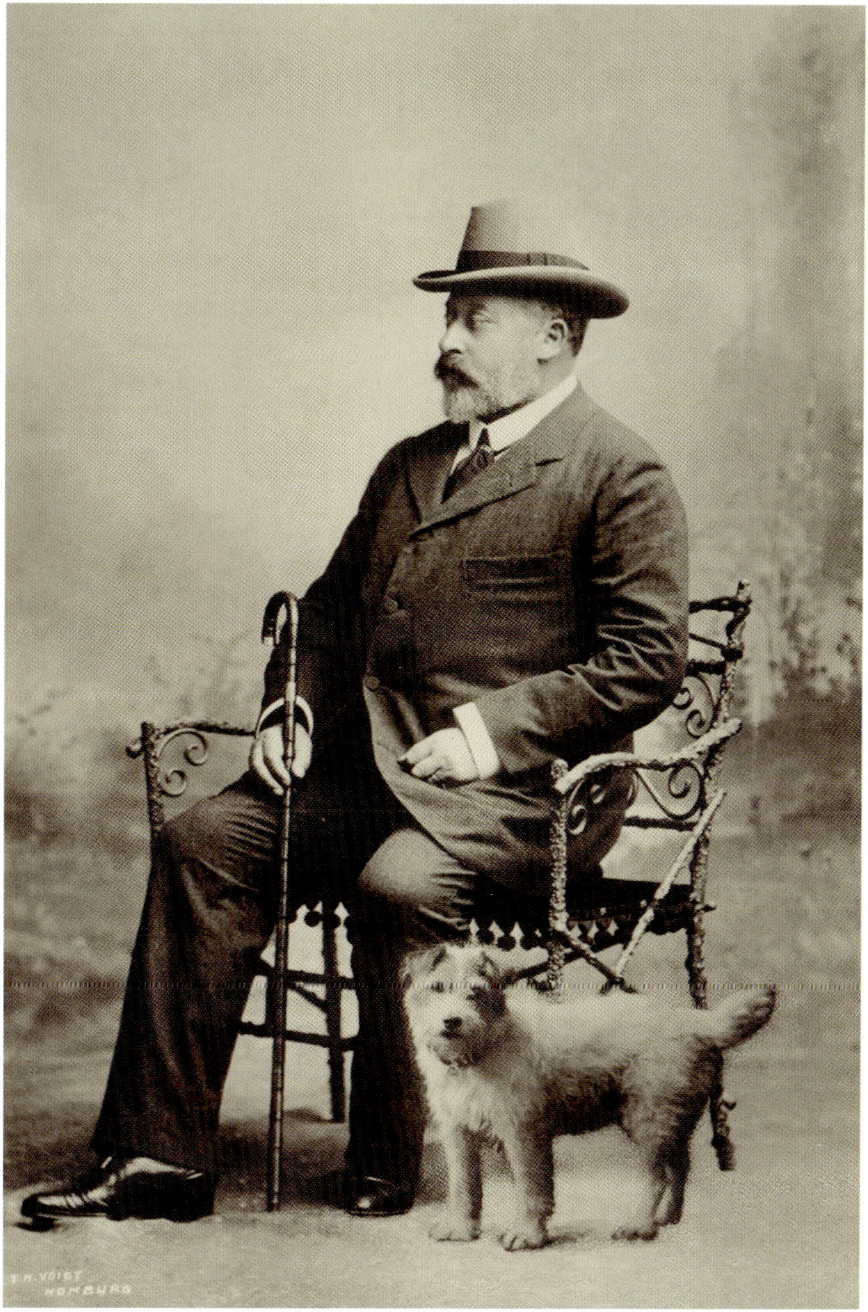

Edward VII (1841–1910) by
Thomas Heinrick Voigt, c.1910.
Sepia glossy postcard print,
125 x 81mm. NPG x39946

BEATRICE HARRISON

Dorothy Wilding, 1923

Even considering the extraordinary proliferation of musical siblings in the early part of the century (the D'Aranyi sisters for example), the four Harrison sisters remain quite exceptional. Beatrice was the outstanding British cellist of her generation, often ranked at the time with Pablo Casals. Her older sister, Margaret, was a pianist and violinist, the third sister, May, an exceptional violinist and the youngest, Monica, a singer. Beatrice was on intimate terms both with the Royal Family and with leading composers of the day: Bax and Delius wrote cello concertos for her, and Delius his double concerto for her and for May, who were both also celebrated for their interpretation of the Brahms double concerto.

In 1923, shortly before this photograph was taken, the family moved to a house near Oxted in Surrey, where Beatrice discovered that there were nightingales in the wood at the bottom of the garden and, more excitingly, that she could accompany them on her cello while they sang. The BBC agreed to attempt an outside broadcast, which was finally successful in May 1924 and caused a sensation. In her autobiography, Beatrice devotes more attention to the nightingales than to her dogs, of which she admits to sixteen in the household, along with assorted reptiles, birds, seven cats, a parrot and a donkey. Described somewhat coyly as 'a pupil' when the shot was published in *Tatler*, this nameless black Scottie was obviously a special favourite and appears with her in another photo of about this time, taken in the garden. After the Second World War, and when her concert career was in decline, Beatrice joined her sister Margaret and a friend in breeding Irish wolfhounds.

Beatrice Harrison (1892–1965) by Dorothy Wilding, 1923. From an original negative (showing the photographer's cropping instructions). NPG x36710

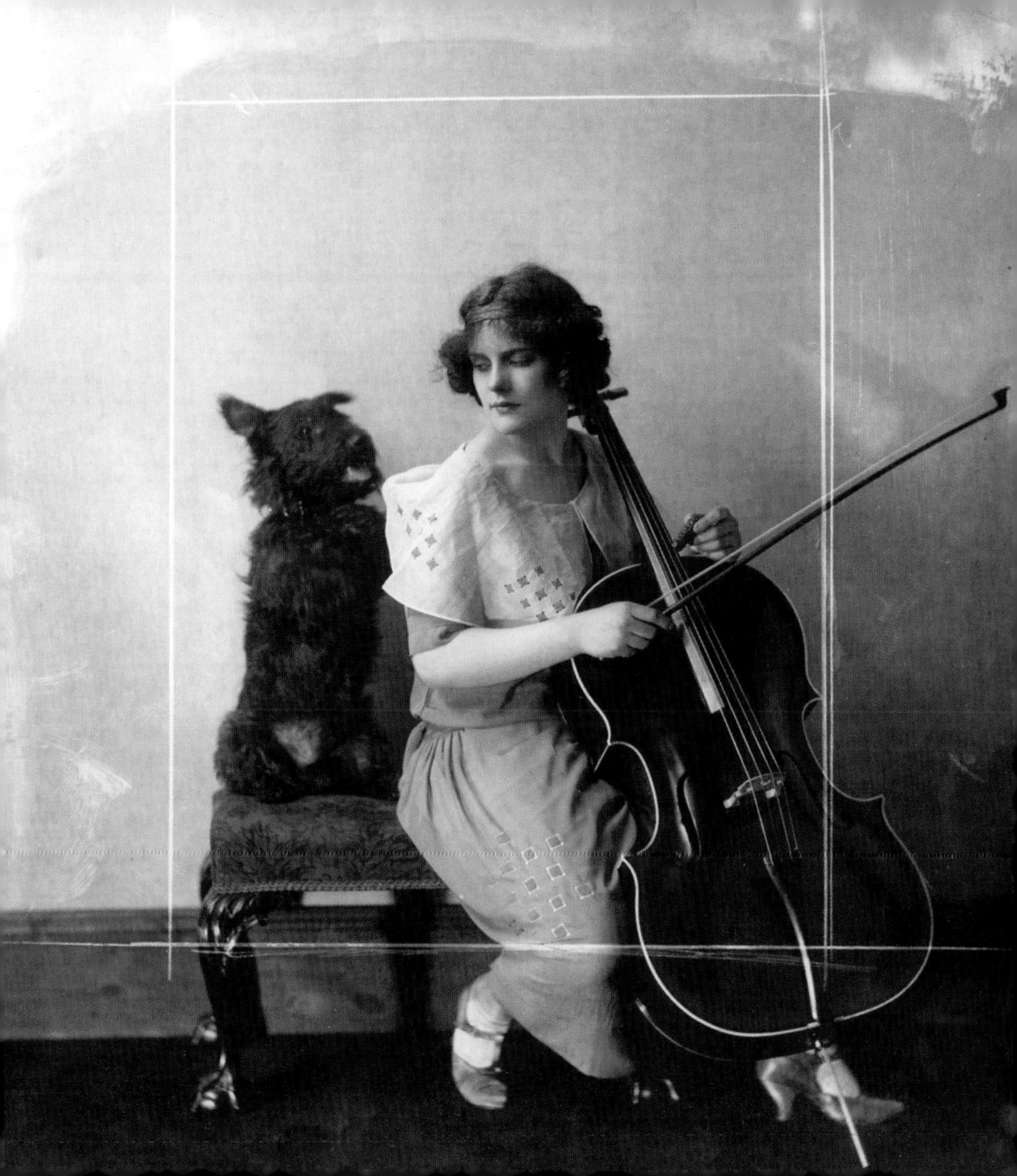

ANNA PAVLOVA WITH JACK

Lafayette, 1927

A legend in her own lifetime, the famous Russian dancer was prima ballerina at the Imperial Ballet in St Petersburg by the age of twenty-five. Pavlova spent one season with Serge Diaghilev's Ballets Russes in 1909 and then created her own company, touring the world until she finally burnt herself out and died before reaching fifty. If she had a home anywhere, it was at Ivy House in Golders Green, London, a palatial villa with a park-sized garden, where she returned every year for a brief resting period and where she kept her theatrical costumes and music library in the cellar. There too she created a spectacular garden and kept a collection of her favourite birds. There were dogs as well, notably a Boston terrier named Poppy and a French bulldog named Duke, but, according to her husband's biography, these all fell victim to quarantine regulations on her tours and ended up being parked on friends in various parts of the world.

Pavlova's most famous solo was 'The Dying Swan', originally choreographed for her by Mikhail Fokine in 1905, and in which she was painted by Sir John Lavery for the once well-known picture in the Tate Gallery. It was perhaps inevitable that an admirer would present her with a pair of mute swans, and Jack and his mate arrived soon after she had acquired Ivy House with its specially enlarged lake in 1913. Jack appears to have behaved like any ordinary swan – 'a splendid big bird, but rather bad-tempered and unapproachable' – until after Pavlova's return to Britain in 1918, when an unidentified swan expert offered to tame it. 'The results ... soon showed themselves. Jack became quite tame and his family increased rapidly from two to eight ... [Pavlova] would take him on her knees and twine his neck around hers and Jack would take it all without the slightest protest.' Jack must have been at least

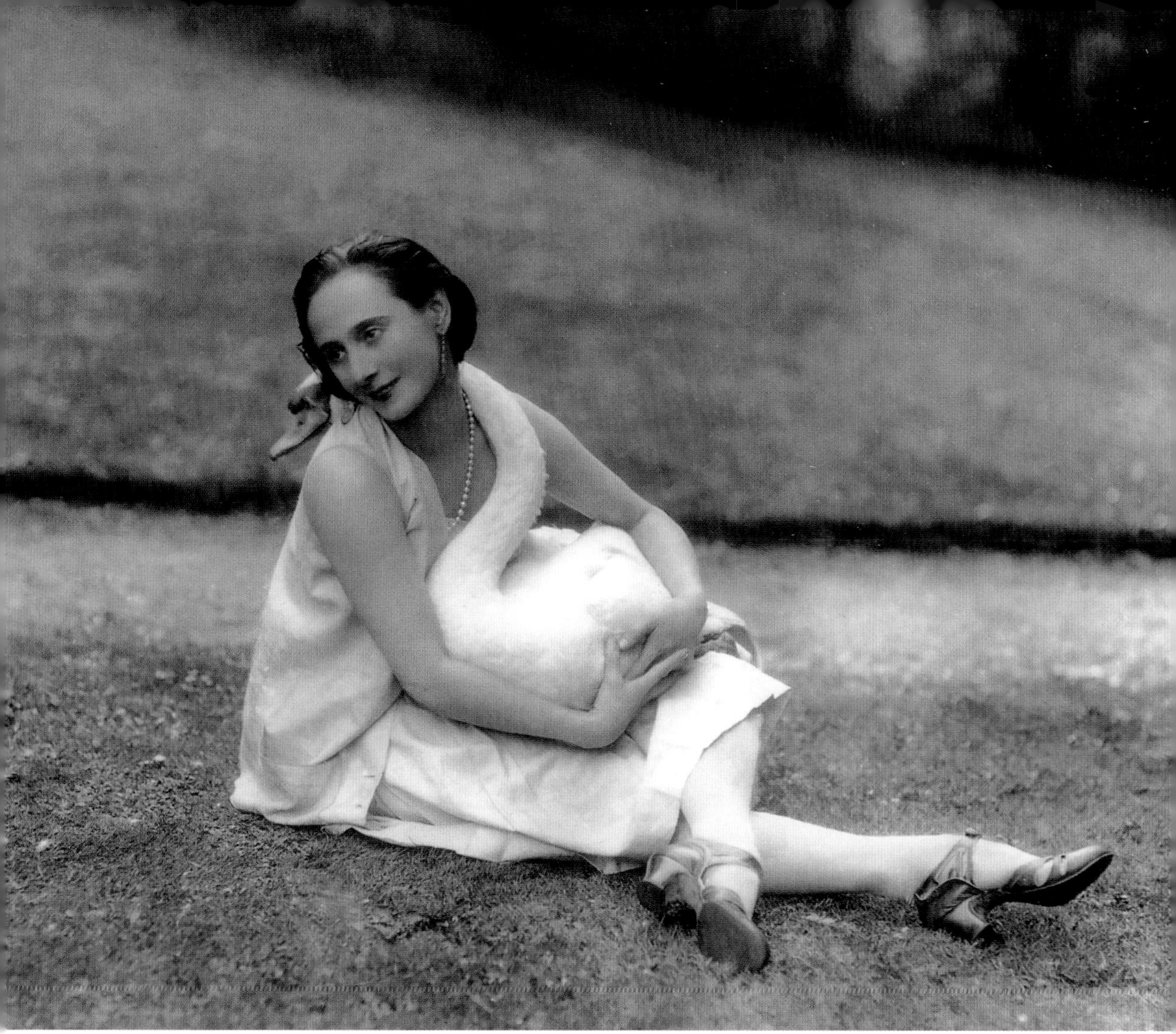

Anna Pavlova (1882–1931) with Jack by Lafayette, 1927. Modern bromide print from original glass negative. NPG x49320

fifteen, a good age for a swan, when this extraordinary photograph was taken, and one cannot help thinking it gives very real substance to the Leda myth. He was succeeded by his son, also named Jack, who outlived their remarkable mistress.

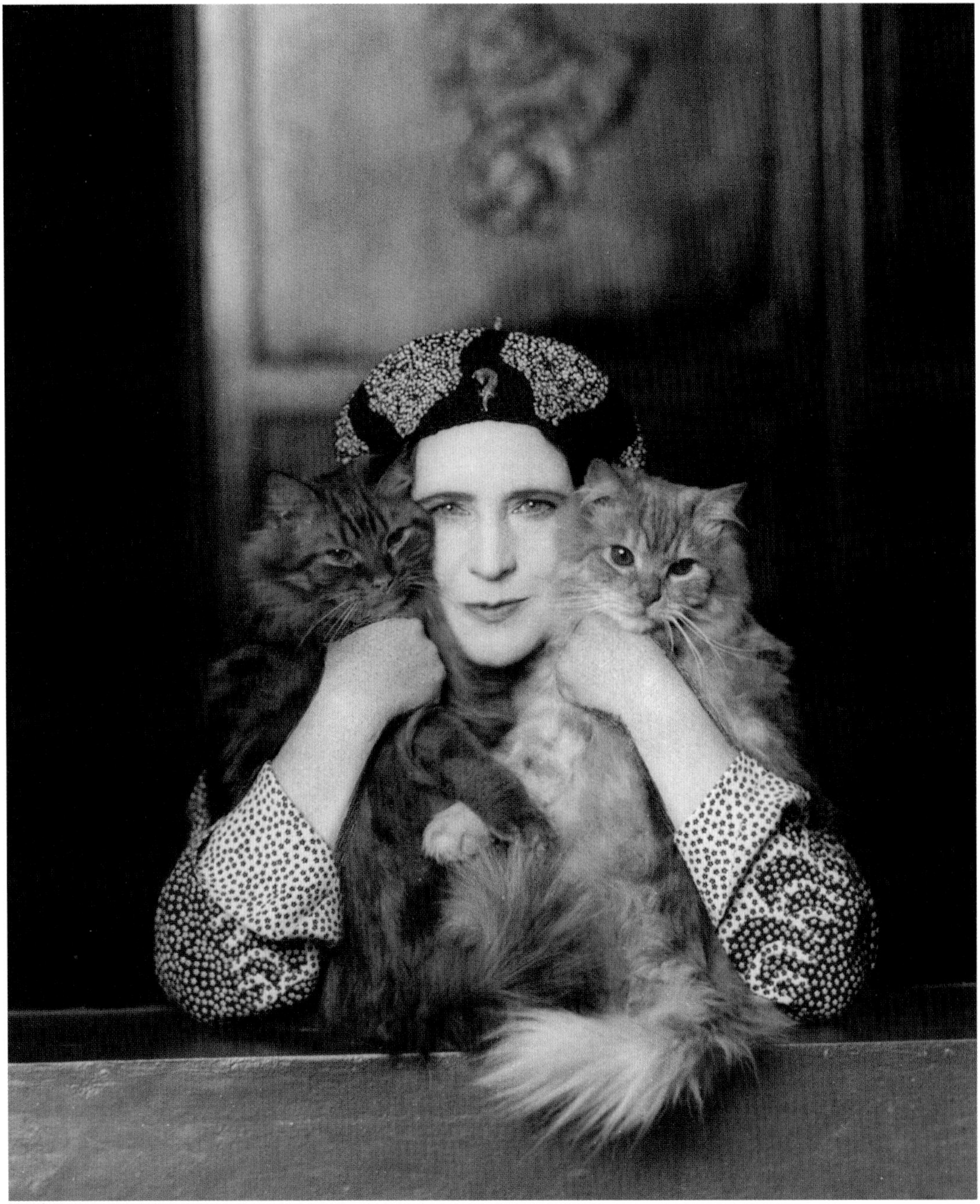

ELINOR GLYN

Paul Tanqueray, 1931

The famous, one might say notorious, novelist is better remembered for her invention of the 'It' factor and for the possibility of sinning with her on a tiger skin than for her novels. Though it portrays her past her first flush of youth, Paul Tanqueray's memorable image conveys something of her intense and passionate nature, which is helpfully underlined by the two cats. In fact, by the time of her demise, she had five tiger skins, three of them named after lovers, though the cats were not acquired until she finally settled back in England in 1929 after seven years in America as a Hollywood scriptwriter for silent films. Even so, at the age of sixty-five she formed her own film-production company in London, though she was obliged to abandon it the following year after the first film received devastating reviews and the second remained unreleased.

The cats were named Candide and Zadig as a tribute to Voltaire, whom Elinor had apparently cherished after finding a copy of his *Zadig* as a little girl in her hated step-father's library in Jersey. Her grandson and biographer, Anthony Glyn, remembered them both (despite the visual evidence) as marmalade-coloured, 'beautiful proud independent creatures of enormous character and "it", in many ways very like their mistress ... they became as much a feature of her life as her tigers'. Indeed, in 1939, Elinor caused a sensation by speaking at a literary lunch at the Dorchester while wearing Candide round her neck as a stole. The cat apparently behaved impeccably.

Elinor Glyn (1864–1943) by Paul Tanqueray, 1931.
Bromide print, 234 x 192mm. NPG x16448

JOHN PIPER

Peggy Angus, 1937

This careful and elegant drawing of the young John Piper is a reminder that in the 1930s he was at the heart of the modern movement in Britain and one of our leading abstract painters. He is sitting on an Alvar Aalto chair (1928) and behind him on the wall hangs his *Forms on Dark Blue* (1936), one of his largest and most important works of the period. The artist, Peggy Angus, was married at the time to Piper's friend and collaborator, the architectural historian J.M. Richards. As editor of the *Architectural Review*, Richards commissioned articles and reviews from Piper, and in 1946 Piper illustrated Richards's study of suburban architecture, *The Castles on the Ground*. Piper was already working on the *Shell Guide to Oxfordshire* (1938) and with the publication of *Brighton Aquatints*, in 1939, his transformation into the most significant British landscape and topographical artist of the century was complete. The one consistent fact about the huge variety of Piper's evocative landscape paintings is that they include neither people nor animals. It is unclear where this portrait is set, so the ownership of the ginger cat on his lap seems likely to remain unknown. The background may be his own house with the still unsold painting; it may be the Richards's, it may be Serge Chermayeff's (Piper did a television programme with him on *Art and Modern Architecture* that January), or it may be purely imaginary, a suitable setting for a leading modernist. Whoever the cat belonged to and whether it invited itself into the picture or not, its role is clearly to add another element of the characterisation of Piper the man: modernists are not all bug-eyed monsters – sometimes they even like cats (and wear carpet slippers)!

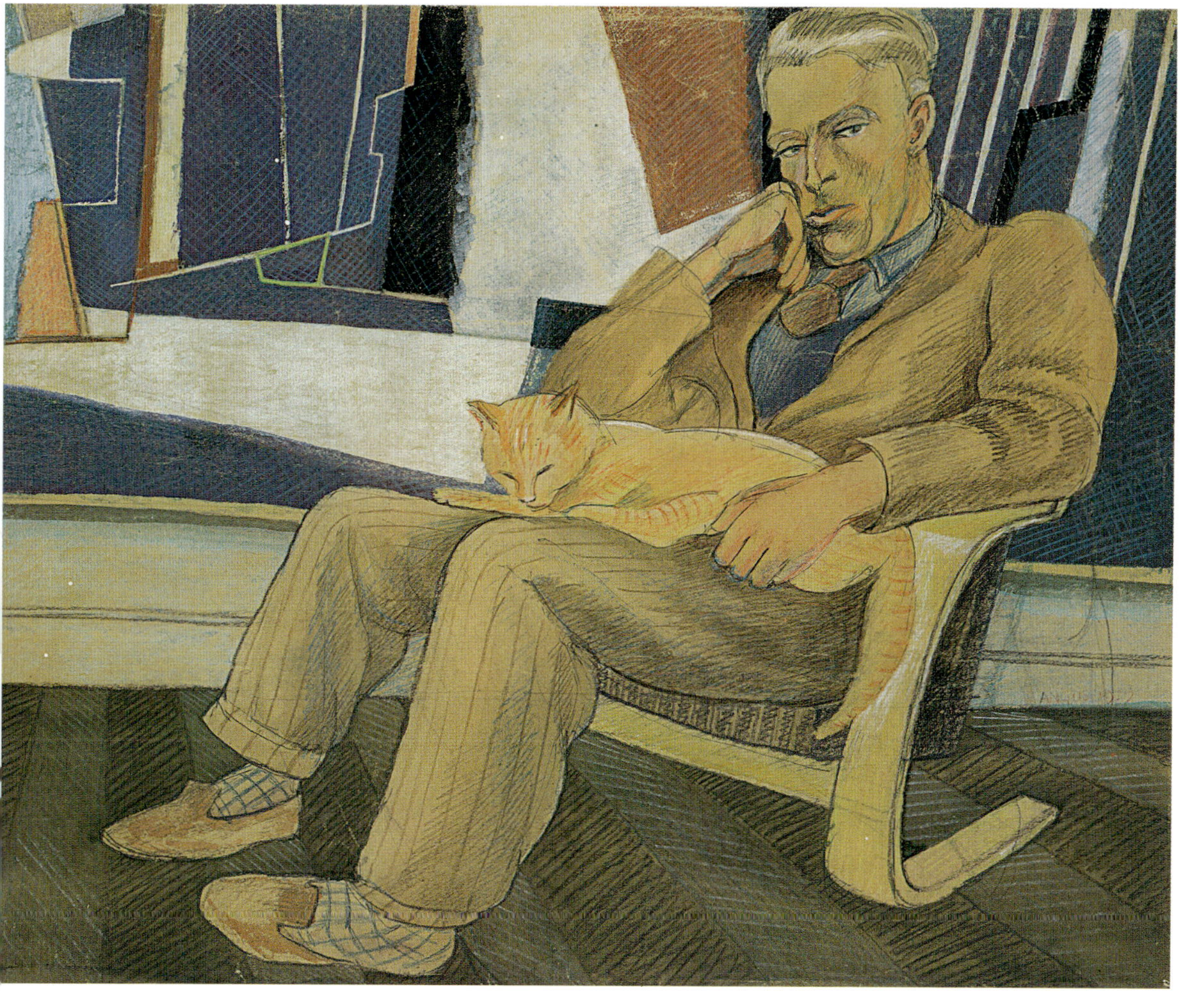

John Piper (1903–92) by Peggy Angus, 1937. Pencil, crayon and wash, 521 x 625mm. NPG 6545

VITA SACKVILLE-WEST AND MARTHA

John Gay, 1948

Daughter of Lord Sackville and brought up at Knole, one of the largest country houses in England, Vita Sackville-West is better known for her unconventional marriage to the diplomat Sir Harold Nicolson and for the creation of the garden at Sissinghurst, where this photograph was taken, than as the prolific writer she had been since childhood. She had won the Hawthornden Prize for her long poem 'The Land' in 1927 and in 1930 became a best-selling author with her novel *The Edwardians*, still valued and read as a record of pre-First World War life in a great country house. Her literary career was interrupted by passionate affairs with a number of women, including Violet Trefusis and Virginia Woolf, but after moving to Sissinghurst in 1930 she became increasingly involved in the creation of the famous garden, contributing a gardening column to the *Observer*, from 1946 to 1961, which was subsequently successfully anthologised.

Her contemporary literary reputation may be gauged from the fact that John Gay took this photograph, published in July 1948, for a series of profiles of poets in *The Strand Magazine*. The dignified and monumental combination of the statuesque figure, the ancient arch and urn and the noble dog conceals a hidden tragedy, for Martha, the German shepherd dog (then known as an Alsatian), was already dying. Vita's companion of thirteen years, Martha had kept her company during Nicolson's weekly absences in London and the war years but in April that year had suffered a heart attack. Harold had arrived to 'find Viti [*sic*] pacing by the lake in an agony of tears'. On 17 June, Vita wrote to him, tormented by the eternal dilemma of whether to have Martha put down: 'when she comes and rests her nose on my knee and looks up at [me] with her golden eyes, so trustful, it makes me feel a traitor ... You see I am essentially a lonely person, and Martha has meant so much to me. She was always there and I could tell her everything.' Three days later Martha was dead, buried in the wood at Sissinghurst, and Vita went to collect an Alsatian puppy called Rollo. A week later, this photo appeared. Vita's last published work was *Faces: Profiles of Dogs* (1961), in which she remembered both her own and her friends' dogs: the saluki that Gertrude Bell had given her in Baghdad ('without exception the dullest dog I ever owned'), Ethel Smyth's Old English sheepdogs, and, of course, her beloved Alsatians.

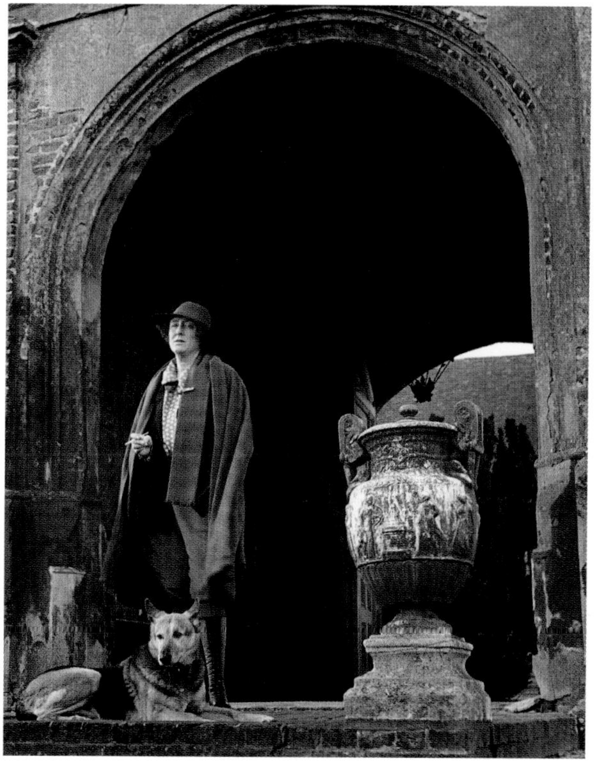

Vita Sackville-West (1892–1962) and Martha by John Gay, 1948. Bromide fibre print, 290 x 224mm. NPG x47302

SIR ALFRED MUNNINGS

Baron, 1954

The only really successful British sporting painter of modern times, Munnings nevertheless worked in a derivation of Impressionism that he had learnt from his great hero, John Singer Sargent. He lived at Dedham in the heart of Constable country, was a keen horseman and spent as much time at Newmarket as he did in his studio. Many of the most famous horses of the day, including Humorist, Hyperion and Brown Jack, were immortalised in his paintings. In 1949 he became perhaps the most controversial president of the Royal Academy ever, and his frequent attacks on modern art did much to enhance the Academy's reputation as a bastion of conservatism.

The photograph was taken in his studio, at the same time as one for *Tatler* magazine published in October 1954, and shows on the wall behind him his recently completed painting *Who's the Lady? HRH Princess Mary*, which was exhibited at the Royal Academy the following year. Photographs of Munnings and Lady Munnings invariably show them with three or four dogs, but apart from his white mongrel Toby, to whom he devotes a lengthy eulogy, only a few of them are identified in his three-volume autobiography. This lively dog appears to be a Labrador retriever with a bit of greyhound in him and is perhaps the same dog that stands in for Munnings in the satirical painting *Does the Subject Matter?*, an attack on modern art and on Sir John Rothenstein, then Director of the Tate Gallery, which caused a storm of controversy two years later.

Sir Alfred Munnings (1879–1959) by Baron (Sterling Henry Hahum), 1954. Bromide print, 175 x 145mm. NPG x21456

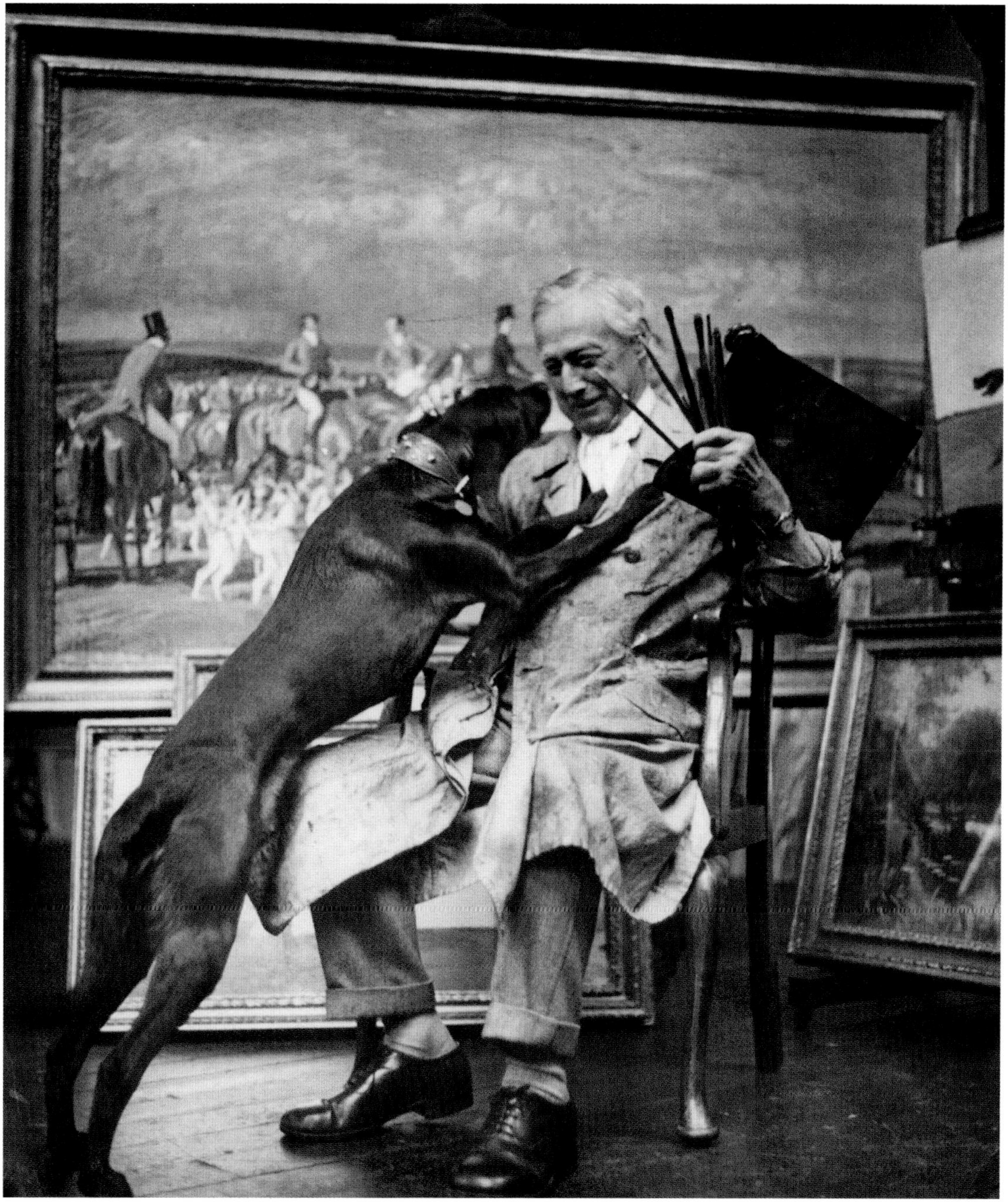

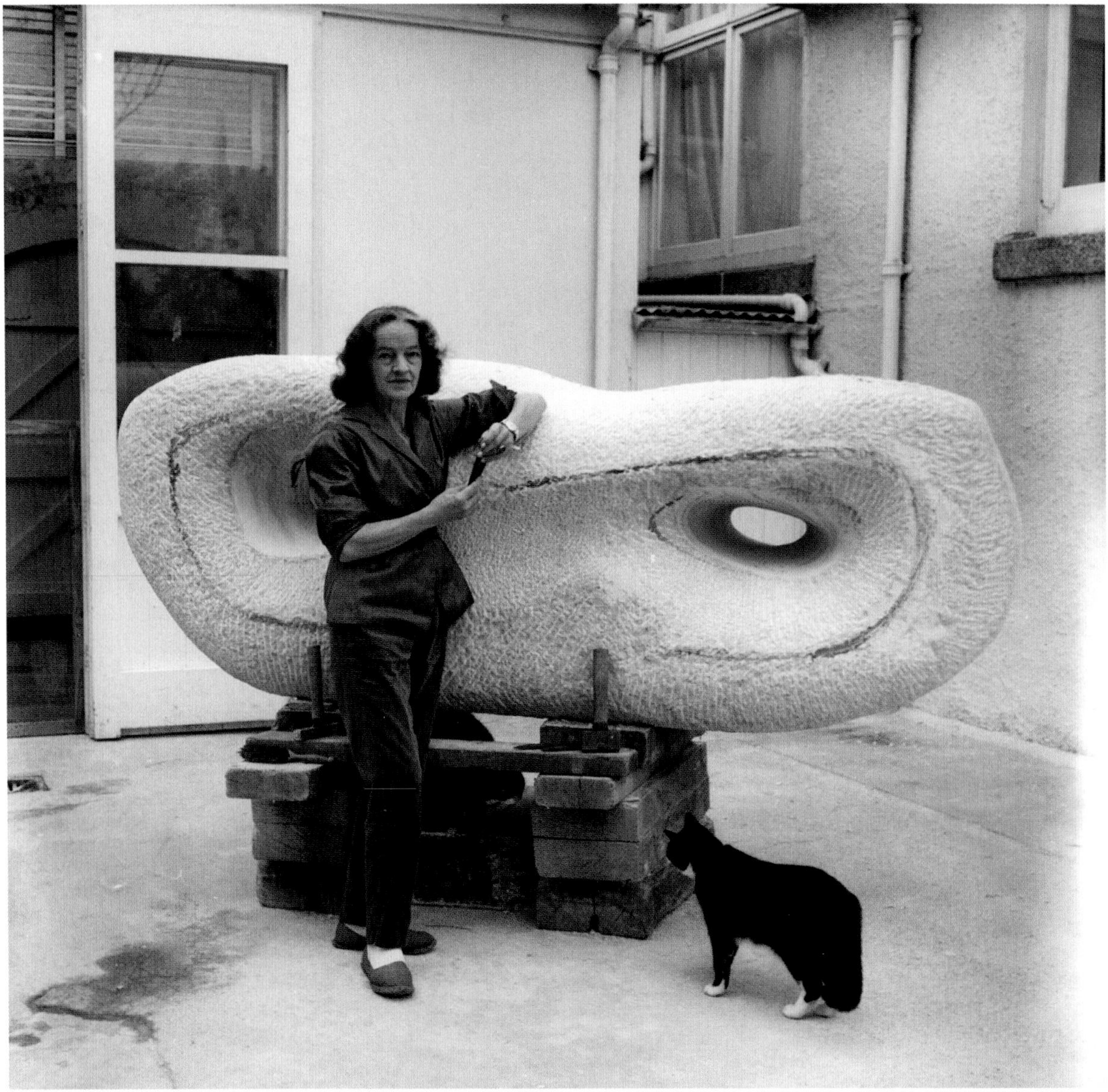

Barbara Hepworth (1903–75) with her cat Nicholas and her sculpture 'Curved Reclining Form (Rosewall)' by Ida Kar, 1961. From an original 2¼-inch square film negative. NPG x31619

BARBARA HEPWORTH

Ida Kar, 1961

By the time the Russian-born photographer Ida Kar went down to St Ives to photograph Barbara Hepworth in her studio, the sculptress was already a figure of more than national significance. Her work had been included in the 1951 Venice Biennale and had also figured prominently in the Festival of Britain the same year. In 1952 a monograph with an introduction by her friend Sir Herbert Read had been published, and she had made a considerable impression as a stage designer for *Electra* at the Old Vic. A major 1954 retrospective at the Whitechapel Gallery in London did much to consolidate her reputation.

Hepworth had moved to St Ives in 1939 and finally settled at Trewyn Studio in 1951 after her divorce from the painter Ben Nicholson. The photograph shows her in the carving yard with the sculpture 'Curved Reclining Form, (Rosewall)', named after the hill outside St Ives from which she had conceived the work. It was purchased in 1962 for a piazza in a draughty civic development by the post office in Chesterfield.

With her children now grown up, and living on her own at the studio, cats seem to have played an increasingly important part in Barbara Hepworth's life. Three of them, Nicholas, Mimi and Tobey, are represented by their own photographs in her *A Pictorial Autobiography*, first published in 1970. A slightly overweight Nicholas, who was clearly a feature of studio life in the 1950s and early 1960s, is seen here making a surreptitious bid for inclusion in the limelight, and he appears again in a photograph of the finished sculpture in the garden at Trewyn.

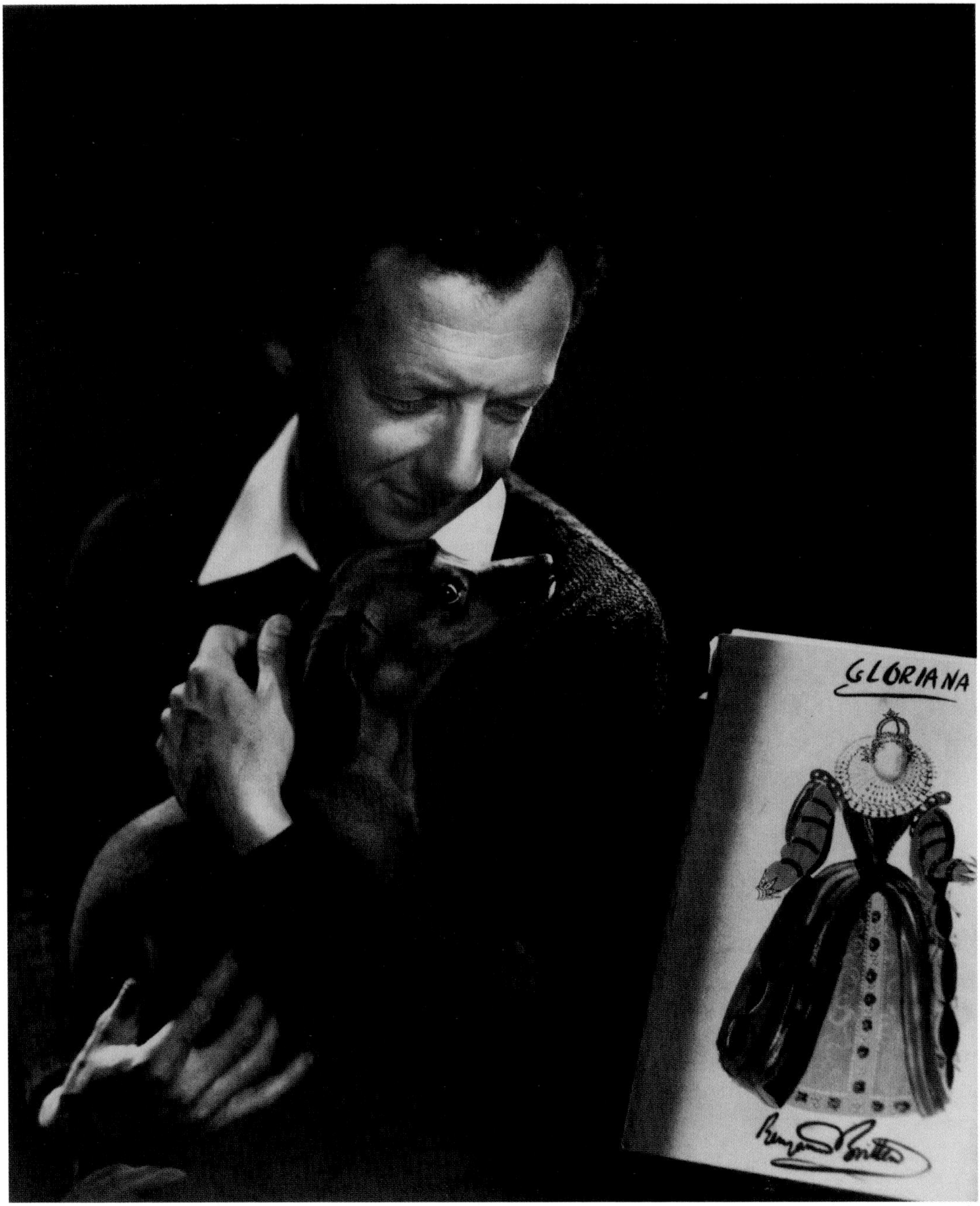
GLORIANA

BENJAMIN BRITTEN

Yousuf Karsh, 1954

The son of a Lowestoft dentist, Britten's fame as a composer had rocketed to international levels after the success of his wartime opera *Peter Grimes* (1945) and its three successors, *The Rape of Lucretia* (1946), *Albert Herring* (1947) and the all-male *Billy Budd* (1951). Always drawn to the sea, he settled in 1947 in the Suffolk town of Aldeburgh, where the following year he founded with his lifelong companion, the tenor Peter Pears, the Aldeburgh Festival, which rapidly became a mecca for leading performing artists and audiences from around the world.

Something of a celebrity himself, the Canadian photographer Yousuf Karsh got lost on the way to Aldeburgh in 1954, and with Britten irritated at his late arrival and insisting on playing tennis and going for a swim before he could be photographed, the session got off to a poor start. Then, wrote Karsh, 'the dog demanded to become part of the picture. Britten swivelled on the piano seat to make room for his canine collaborator, who leaped into the safety of his arms, while yet casting a wary eye on me.' Thereafter all must have been sweetness and light, for Karsh's two published photographs of Britten are among the best portraits of the composer. The score on the music stand is of his opera *Gloriana* (1953), written for the Coronation of Elizabeth II, and his next, *The Turn of the Screw* (1954), must by then have been in rehearsal for its premiere in Venice that autumn. The little dachshund is almost certainly Clytie, presumably originally Peter Pears's dog since she was named after his American singing teacher, Clytie Mundy, but she had clearly adopted the composer and appears in the portrait of him painted a few years later by their neighbour Mary Potter. By the time the Britten–Pears household moved in 1957 to The Red House, their final residence in Aldeburgh, there were two dachshunds, a situation that seems to have remained constant for the rest of Britten's life.

Benjamin Britten, Baron Britten (1913–76) by Yousuf Karsh, 1954. Bromide print, 339 x 269mm. NPG P490[14]

THE DUKE AND DUCHESS OF WINDSOR WITH DIZZY

Dorothy Wilding, 1955

Dizzy (short for Disraeli) was the first of nine Windsor pugs and joined the Duke and Duchess's household in France soon after their return from wartime governorship of the Bahamas in 1945. With them had come Pookie, last in line of a succession of cairn terriers that had begun with Slipper, whom the Duke, then Edward, Prince of Wales, had presented to the Duchess, then Wallis Simpson, for Christmas 1934. The Duke had clearly inherited the Royal Family's love of dogs, apparent from his grandmother Queen Victoria onwards, and Slipper appears in a number of pre-war photographs by Dorothy Wilding, both with him and with the Duchess. Slipper rather ominously died of a snake bite shortly after the Abdication in 1936 and before the fateful wedding.

Responsibility for usurping the cairn terriers' hold on the Windsors' affections clearly lies with Dizzy, and they took to pugs with something of an obsession. In the sale catalogue of the Windsors' effects were several silver-plated dog bowls, engraved collars, pug bed-linen and a whole host of 'puggiana', including paintings and Meissen figurines. This photograph was taken in Dorothy Wilding's studio in New York, where the Windsors had an apartment and where their pugs were often proudly paraded in national dog shows.

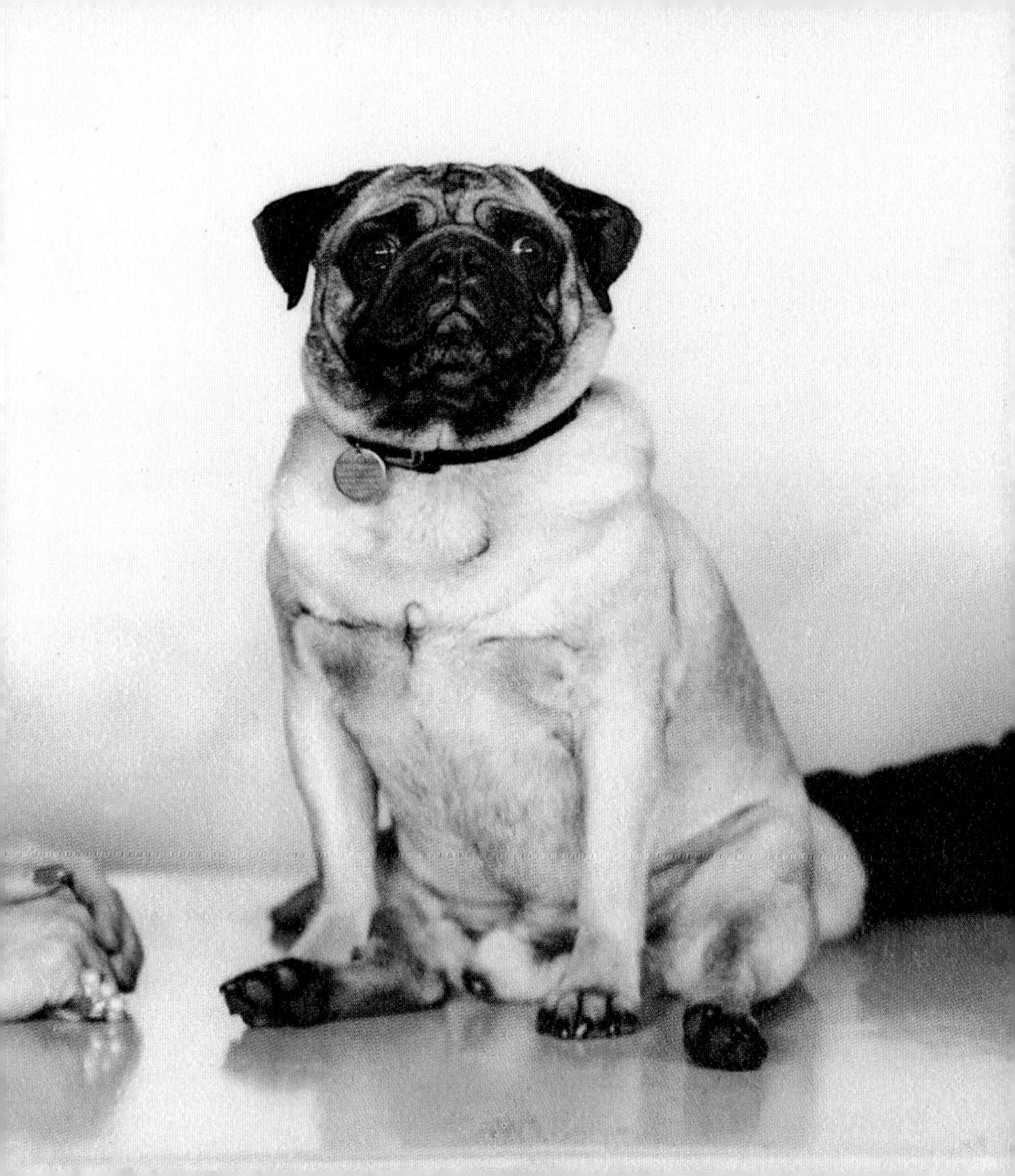

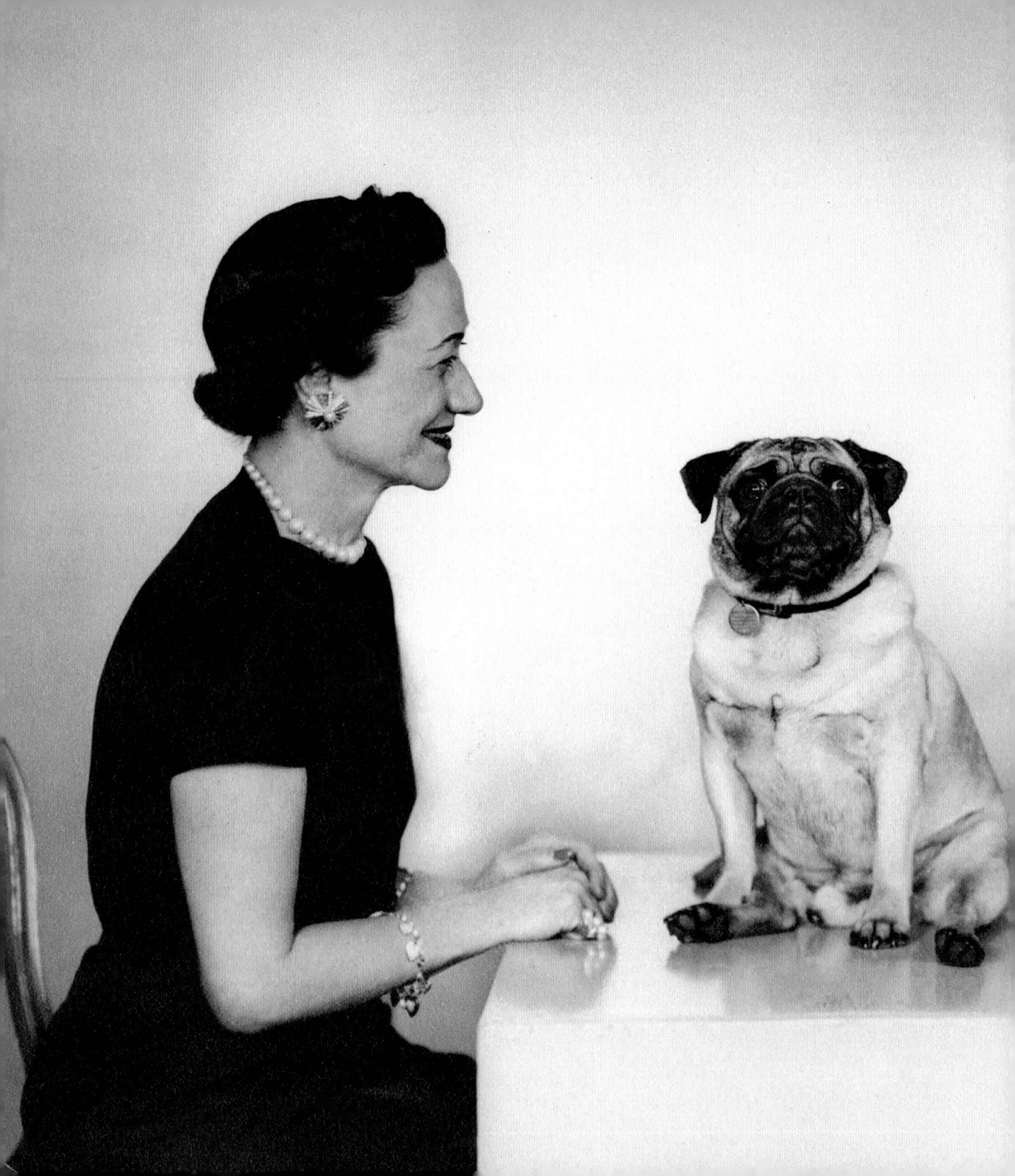

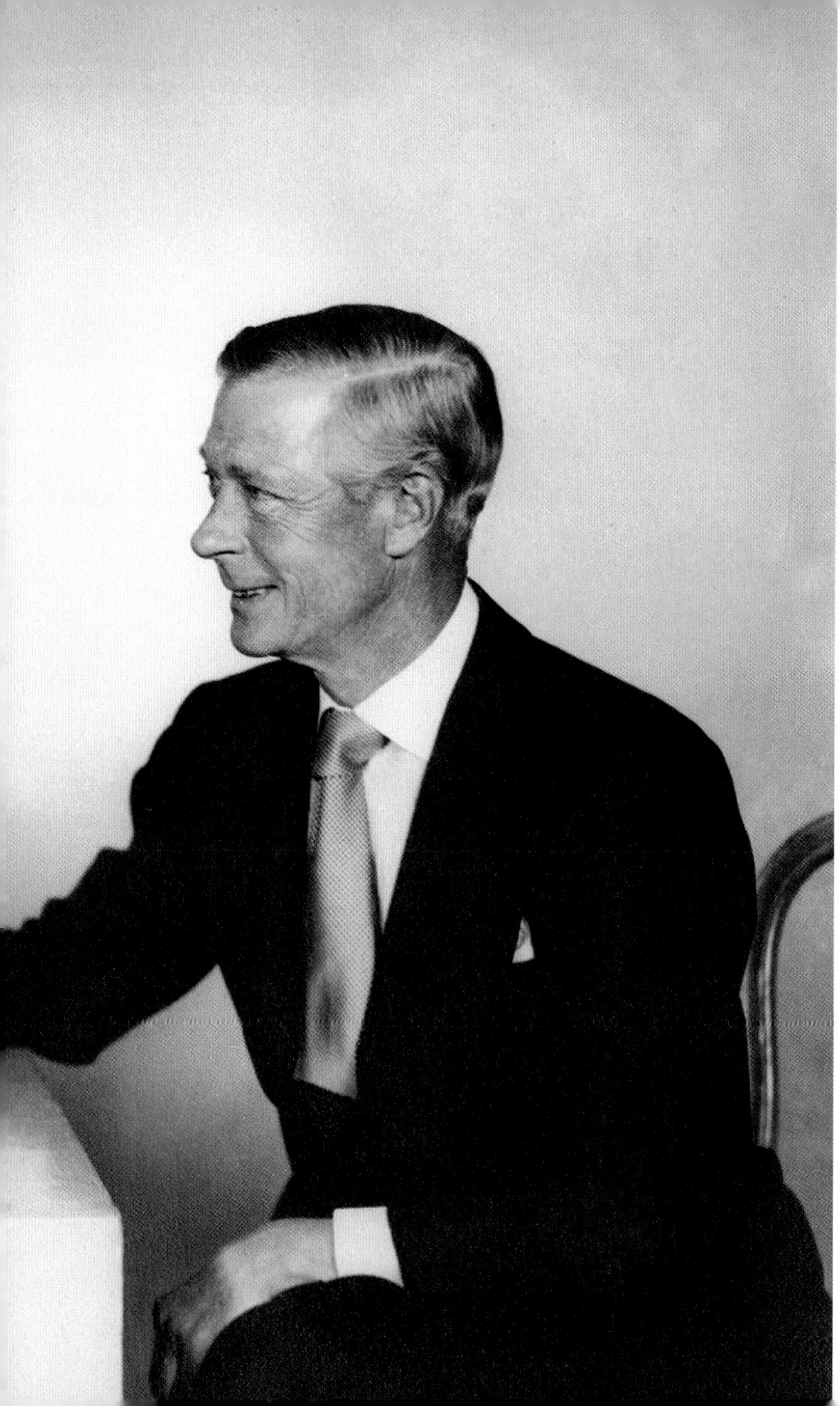

The Duke (1894–1972) and Duchess (1896–1986) of Windsor with Dizzy by Dorothy Wilding, 1955. Toned bromide print, 161 x 239mm. NPG x27966

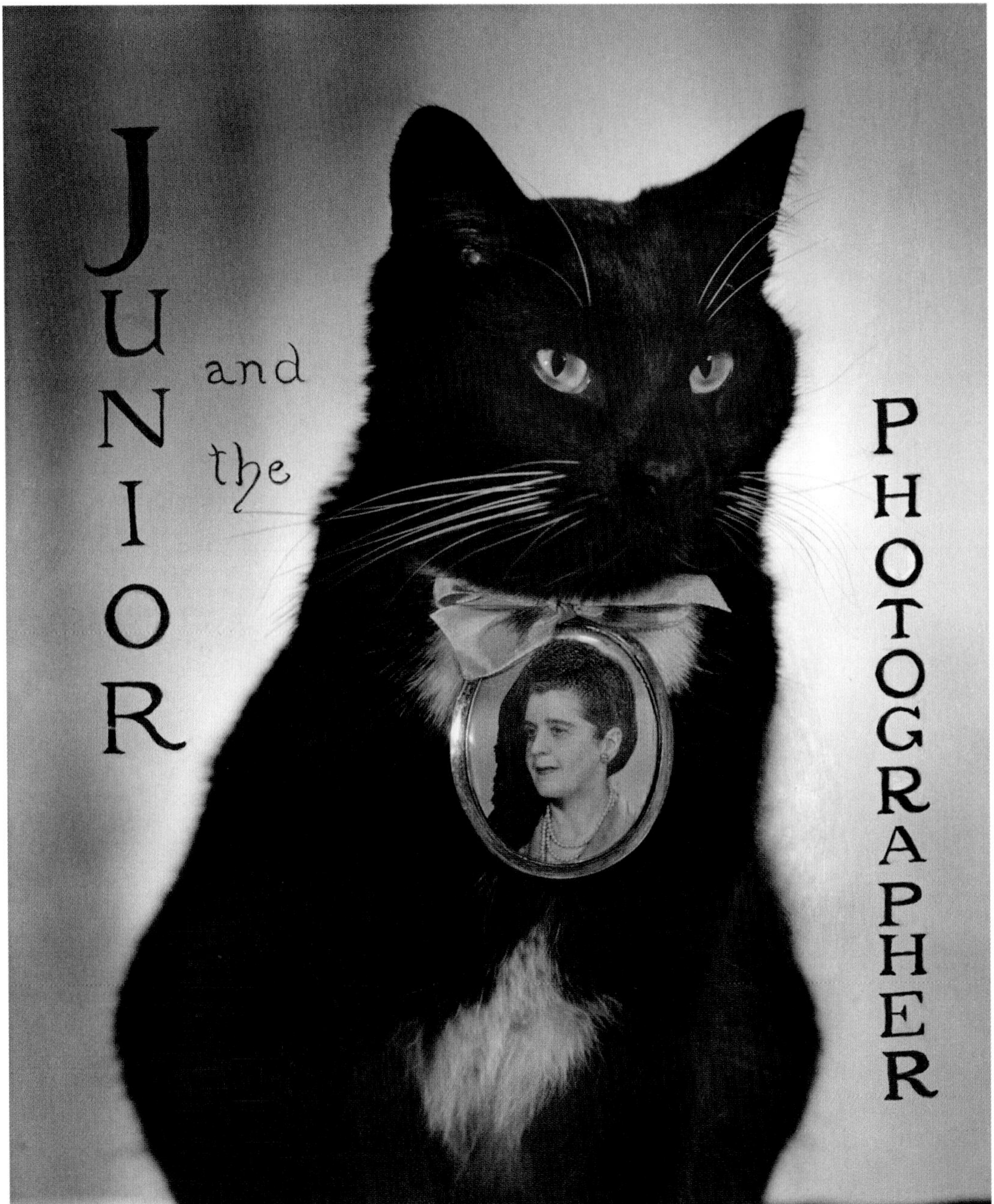
JUNIOR
and
the
PHOTOGRAPHER

MADAME YEVONDE

Self-portrait, c.1958

Although still a little-known name, Madame Yevonde (she was born Yevonde Cumbers) was one of the most colourful and original figures in British photography. Her pioneering work with colour photography in the 1930s was extremely influential and has scarcely been equalled since. This entertaining self-portrait is typical of her always inventive approach to the medium and surely indicative of the importance cats played in her life. She had been happily married to a minor playwright called Edgar Middleton and was devastated by his premature death in 1939. Although not mentioned at all in her entertaining biography, *In Camera* (1940), it was her cats who seem increasingly to have filled the void left by his death.

The cats had the free run of her studio. Whiskey wormed his way into several of her society portraits in the 1930s, and it was probably he who managed to escape with her to safety seconds before a direct hit on her Berkeley Square studio during the Blitz. Junior also appears in other photographs. On the reverse of the mount, Mme Yevonde has inscribed: 'JUNIOR – Winner of the 1958 Good Conduct Prize offered by the Cats Protection League for the most distinguished cat. He was aged 18 when he disappeared. He is wearing a very early photograph of the photographer.' Modest as always, the photograph in question cannot in fact have been taken much before 1945.

Madame Yevonde (1893–1975), self-portrait (*Junior and the Photographer*), c.1958. Bromide print, 362 x 285mm. NPG x26030

DAME EDITH SITWELL

Mark Gerson, 1962

During her lonely and unloved childhood in the ancestral home at Renishaw, the redoubtable poet often felt that her only friends were the animals and birds she adopted. There was Peaky, the Renishaw peacock with whom she 'walked round ... with my arm around his lovely neck, that shone like tears in a dark forest' until 'my father bought Peaky a wife (in my eyes a most dull and insignificant bird) and he discarded my companionship ... It was my first experience of faithlessness.' There was also a puffin with a wooden leg, and 'a baby owl that had fallen out of its nest, and which used to sleep with its head on my shoulder, pretending to snore in order to attract mice'.

In later life, however, it was cats who shared Dame Edith's life. She was indefatigable in her devotion to them, writing vociferous letters to newspapers and even notes in her address book about cruelty cases. A cat she had had to leave in Paris in 1939 was regularly sent money for his food, and frequent reports on his health were required in return. By 1962 she was living in a flat in Hampstead, north London, with four cats: Shadow, a Siamese, two adopted strays, Orion and Belaker, and her favourite, the cream-coloured Leo.

The photographer Mark Gerson, who came to photograph Dame Edith for an article in *Books and Bookmen*, also photographed Leo on his own. 'You have made him look so majestic', she wrote, thanking him for his gift, 'that I think, no matter how fine your photographs of me may be, it is *Leo* who ought to figure on the cover of *Books and Bookmen*.' As it is, the glimpse of wheelchair, Dame Edith's still powerful profile and Leo's gentle acquiescence add up to a touching image of resilience in old age and fading greatness.

Dame Edith Sitwell (1887–1964) by Mark Gerson, 1962.
Bromide print, 250 x 200mm. NPG x46700

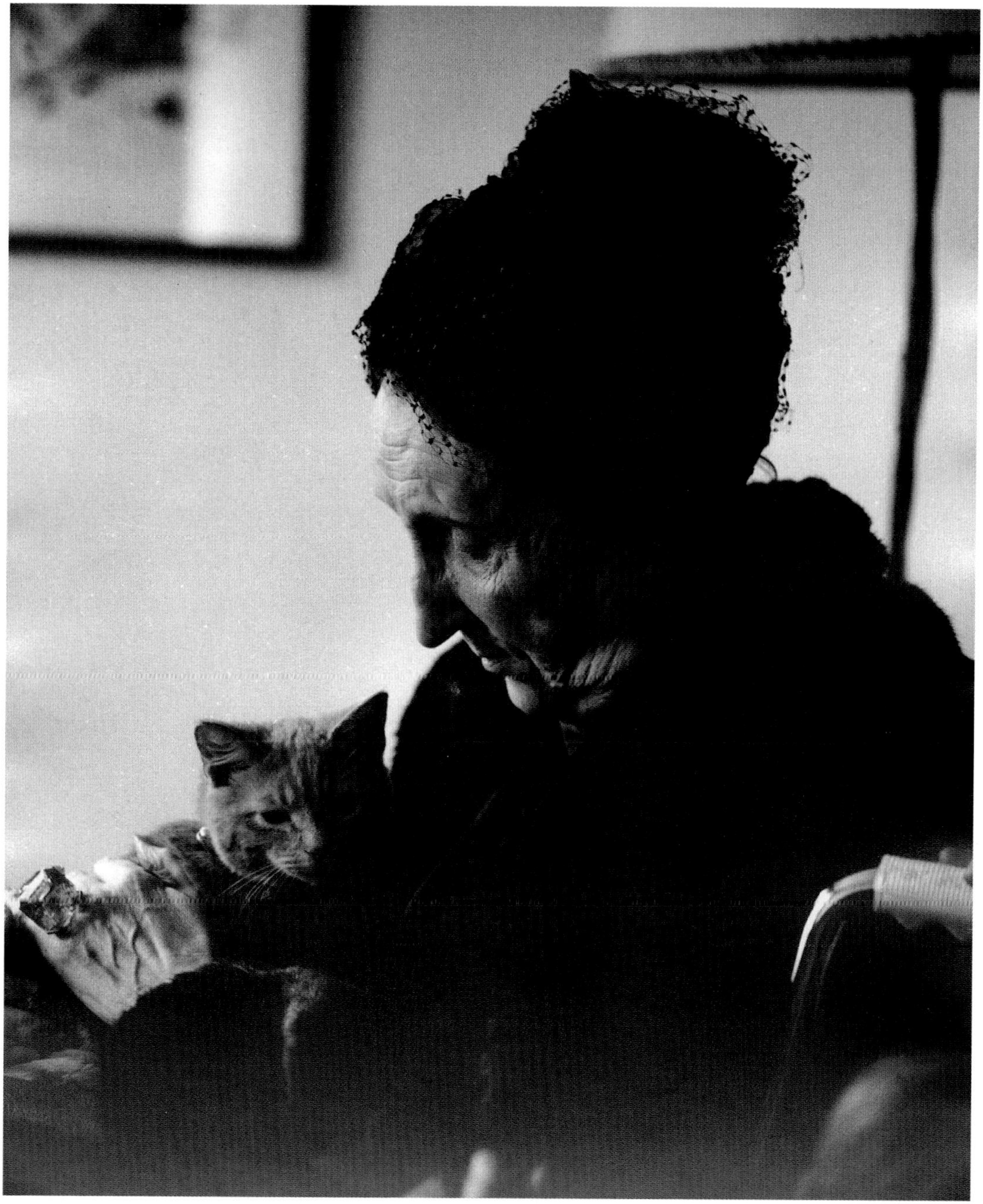

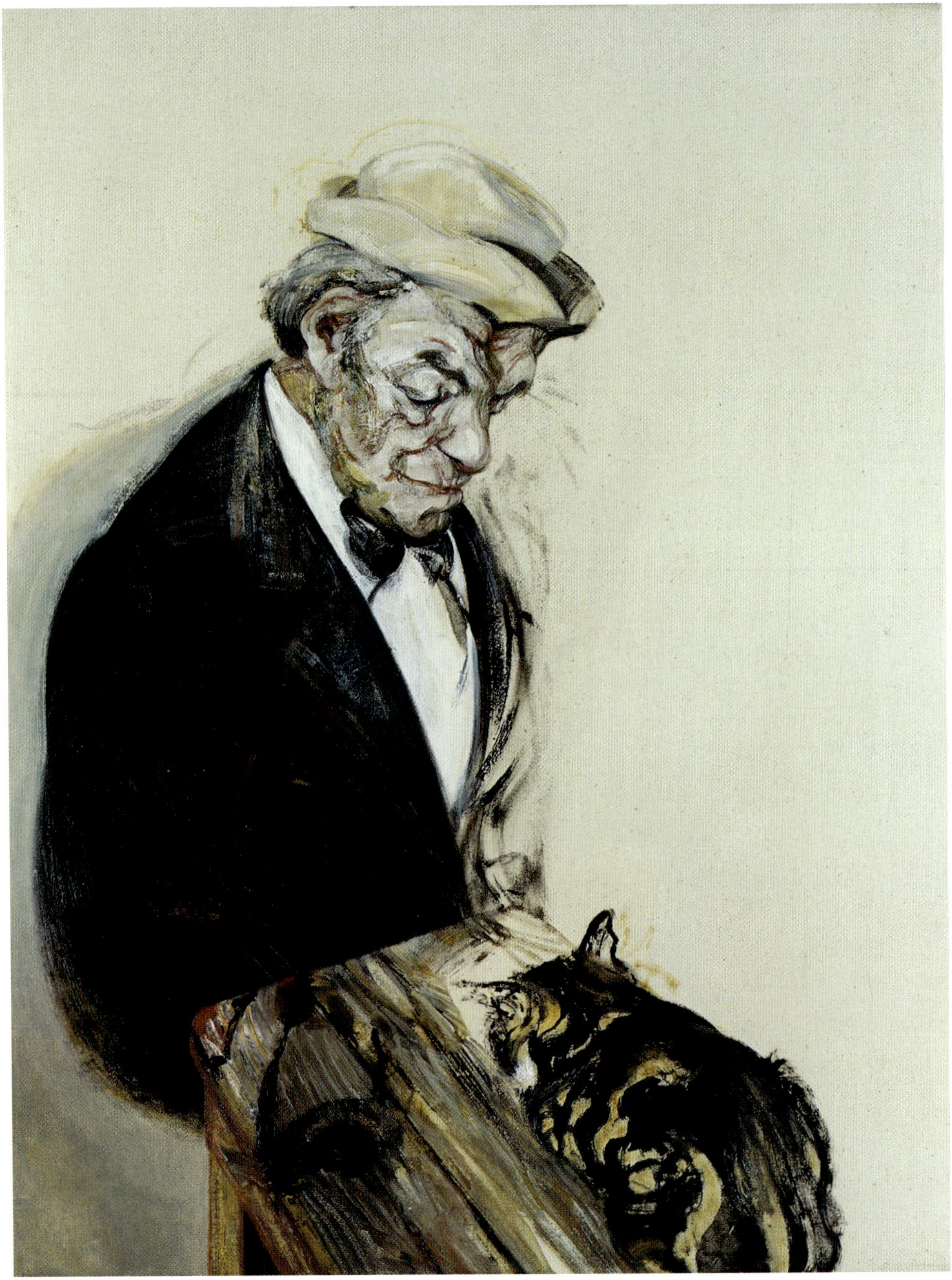

Max Wall (1908–90)
(*Max with Onde*) by
Maggi Hambling,
1981. Oil on canvas,
914 x 660mm.
NPG 5578

MAX WALL WITH ONDE

Maggi Hambling, 1981

For nearly two years of her life, from spring 1981 to early 1983, Maggi Hambling devoted herself almost entirely to fifteen paintings and quite as many drawings of the comedian and entertainer Max Wall. A stand-up comic and entertainer in the old vaudevillian tradition, his career had gone through the doldrums in the 1950s and early 1960s, but by the time she first met him he was, aged seventy-three, increasingly being recognised as a serious actor of considerable power, especially for his appearances in roles like Vladimir in Samuel Beckett's *Waiting for Godot*.

In early 1981, while Maggi was Artist in Residence at the National Gallery, Max was performing in a revival of his one-man show, *Aspects of Max Wall*, across the Charing Cross Road at the Garrick Theatre. She went to see him twice and, bowled over, plucked up courage and wrote to him. The relationship that developed between the 35-year-old artist and the veteran vaudevillian does not, in retrospect, seem surprising to anyone who knows Maggi's single-minded devotion to her work and to her friends. When Max asked her why she was doing all these paintings of him, she could only reply, 'Because you inspire me.'

The afternoon sittings and late-night drinking and eating (when he was not performing) became a regular feature of her Battersea studio, also shared by her three cats. Onde, Onde's brother Parole and Mr Smith all put in an appearance in one or other of the widely diverse and imaginative Max Wall paintings.

Max with Onde, the second in the series, is probably the least theatrical and is based on a drawing from the first sittings. During rests, Max would tell stories and jokes, do conjuring tricks and sing songs. The painting captures the moment when he had just finished singing 'Poor Little Rich Girl' to Onde, who had been fussy about eating her tea, the magic of the event still tangible in the air – performer and recipient united in silent reflection. Onde, who had made an earlier appearance in the National Portrait Gallery's self-portrait by Hambling (1977–8), had originally come to stay for six months but remained for the seventeen and a half years of her life. Like many of the animals in Hambling's work, she is here also a personification of the artist.

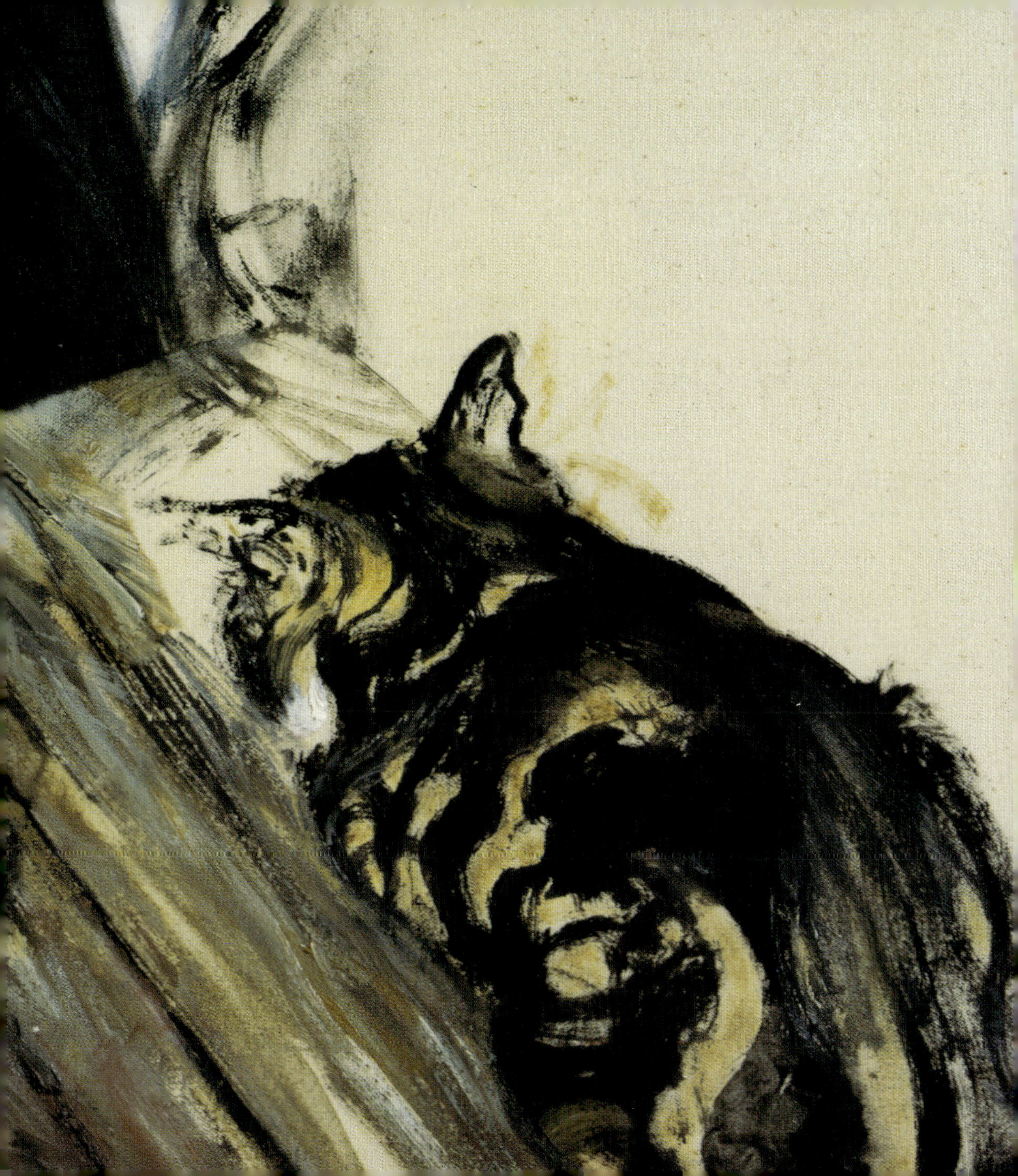

HM QUEEN ELIZABETH II

Michael Leonard, 1985–6

This vivid and cheerful portrait of the Queen was commissioned by *Reader's Digest* magazine from a leading British photorealist painter to celebrate Her Majesty's sixtieth birthday. The artist, Michael Leonard, said that he 'wanted to give the viewer a feeling of having a conversation with the Queen'. Cheered no doubt by having a favourite corgi to share her ordeal and only having to pose for photographs (from which the portrait was painted), this is indeed one of the most extrovert and approachable of all the many paintings that have been made of the Queen. The setting is the Yellow Drawing-room at Buckingham Palace (the same as for Bryan Organ's 1981 portrait of Princess Diana), and the corgi's 'red-gold coat became the colour key for a picture largely made up of variations on gold – a scheme I hoped would help to convey a feeling of royalty combined with human warmth'. The corgi was the 8-year-old Spark, whom the Queen herself chose to bring along to the sittings, 'possibly because of her obedience and good nature ... Spark was a great asset at the sittings. She did all that was asked of her and provided the occasion for Her Majesty to adopt a pose that was unforced and natural, lending the composition a degree of liveliness and movement.'

Spark was not the first royal corgi to appear in a portrait of the Queen at the National Portrait Gallery. One can be seen sleeping on the floor in Sir James Gunn's 1950 *Conversation Piece at the Royal Lodge, Windsor*, a painting of King George VI and his family. It was in 1933, when he was Duke of York, that

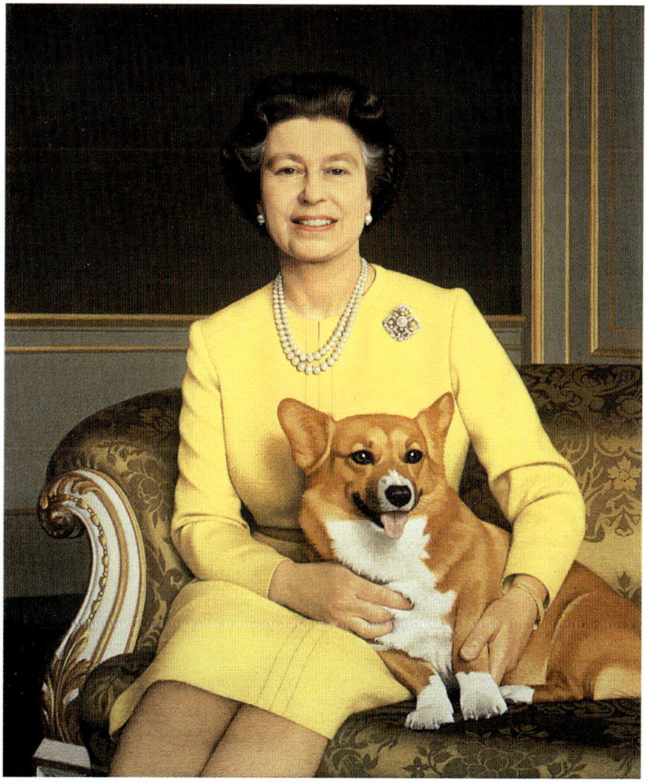

HM Queen Elizabeth II (b.1926) by Michael Leonard, 1985–6. Acrylic on cotton duck, 762 x 616mm. NPG 5861

the King first bought a Pembroke Welsh corgi, called Dookie, as a pet for his two young daughters. Originally used for droving cattle, Pembrokeshire corgis are an ancient Welsh breed and are slightly smaller and – partly due to their royal patronage – better known than Cardigan Welsh corgis. Dookie was joined by Jane in 1938 and soon after by their puppies, Crackers and Carol. The Queen grew up with these corgis, and she has remained attached to them ever since. Spark belonged to the tenth generation of corgis descended from Susan, a bitch from a Cambridgeshire kennels who was given to the Queen for her eighteenth birthday in 1944.

SIR EMMANUEL KAYE

Paul Brason, 1991

Sir Emmanuel Kaye, a noted industrialist and philanthropist, had originally suggested Paul Brason, a former Portrait Award winner, for the job of painting his portrait, since he admired the artist's double portrait of Sir Roy Strong, showing both the professional and the personal sides of the sitter's life. Unwilling to repeat exactly the same formula, Brason suggested the imaginative compromise seen here of using Sir Emmanuel's reflection in the plate-glass window, apparently looking out into the garden towards his beloved golden Labrador, Barley. A connoisseur and collector as well as a keen animal lover, Sir Emmanuel was anxious that the caption on the portrait when it was unveiled should make it clear that the bird in the cage was an antique mechanical canary and not a real one.

Barley was five years old when the portrait was painted and had been acquired from a shop in Sir Emmanuel's local town of Odiham, Hampshire. Labrador retrievers originally developed, as the name suggests, on the coast of Canada, where they were used for helping to haul in the fishermen's nets. Popular as a gun dog since the latter half of the nineteenth century, the breed is known for its responsiveness and in recent years has been much used as a guide dog and for detecting drugs and explosives. Indeed, at the age of one year, Barley himself was pronounced by a leading dog-behaviour specialist to be 'a dream dog'.

Sir Emmanuel Kaye (1914–99) by Paul Brason, 1991.
Oil on canvas, 1068 x 914mm. NPG 6158

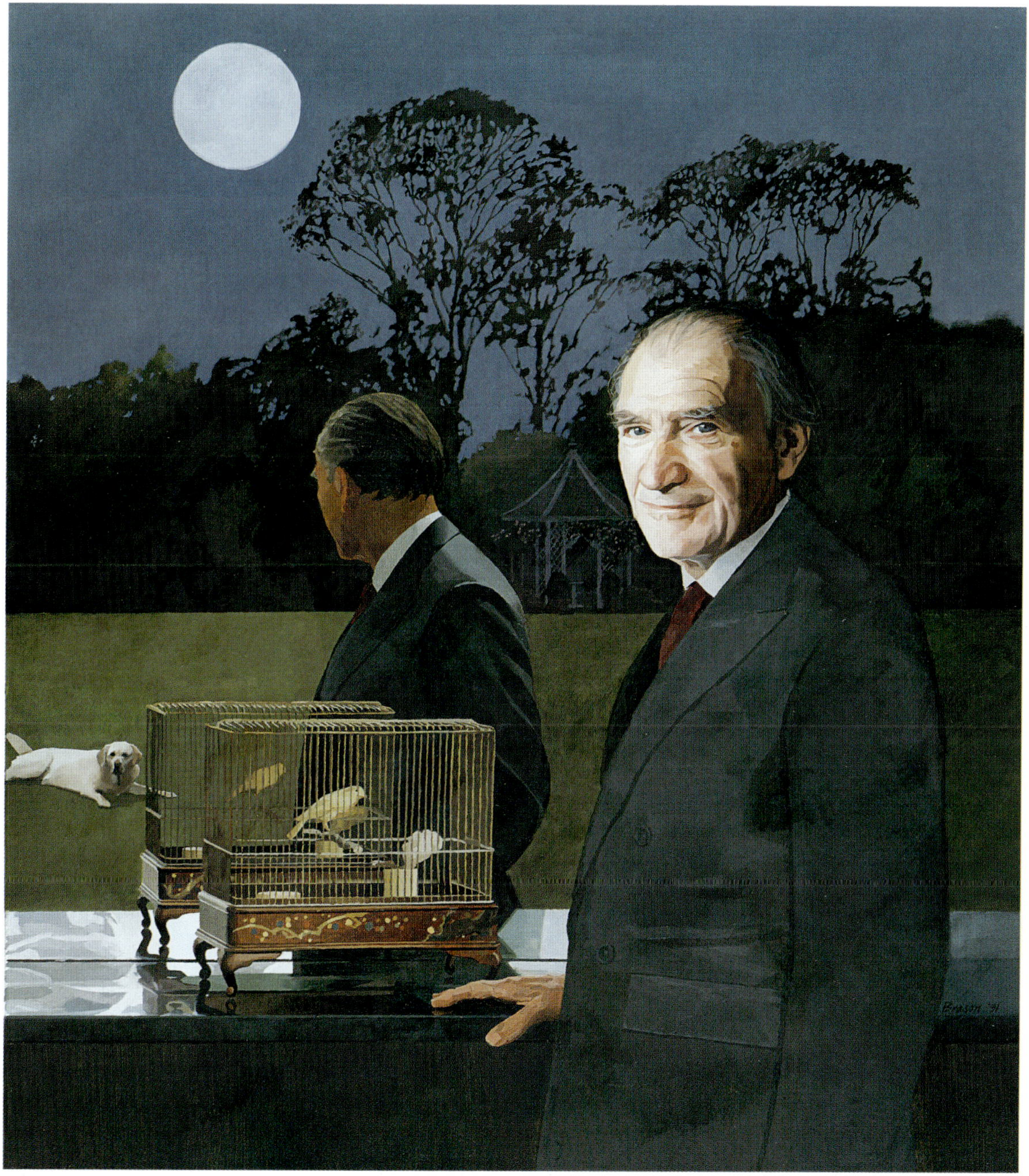

INDEX

Note: page numbers in **bold** refer to captions.

ACKNOWLEDGEMENTS

I am especially grateful to the natural historian and author David Alderton, whose comments on the identification of the various dog breeds were invaluable (and saved me in particular from finding Newfoundlands wherever I looked). I must also thank Maggi Hambling, Sir Emmanuel Kaye and Paul Brason for information on their portraits, and my colleagues at the National Portrait Gallery, especially Catharine MacLeod, Jacky Colliss Harvey and my editor, Ariane Bankes.

Robin Gibson, 1998

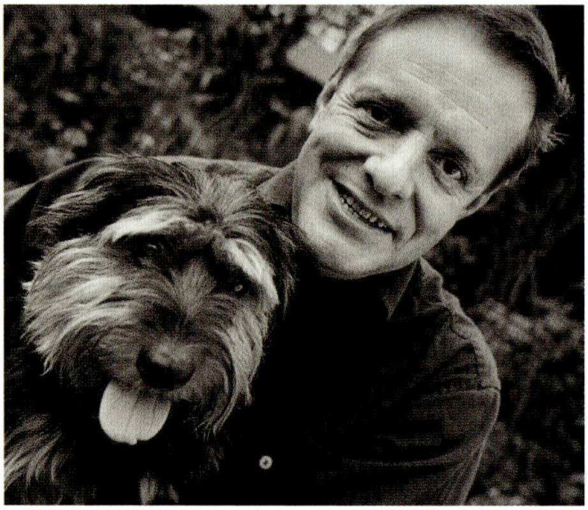

Robin Gibson (1944–2010) with Ted by Nick Sinclair, 1997. Bromide print, 166 x 251mm. NPG x134214

PICTURE CREDITS

Published in Great Britain by National Portrait Gallery Publications,
St Martin's Place, London WC2H 0HE

For a complete catalogue of current publications, please write to the National Portrait Gallery at the address above, or visit our website at www.npg.org.uk/publications

Originally published as *The Face in the Corner* in 1998
This edition, with a new introduction by Chris Packham, published 2015

Note: although some details (including dates of works) have been updated in light of research conducted since 1998, the titles of works used by the author in the original edition of this book, and the order in which they were presented, have been retained.

ISBN 978 1 85514 498 9

10 9 8 7 6 5 4 3 2 1

A catalogue record for this book is available from the British Library.

For the original edition
Publishing Manager: Jacky Colliss Harvey
Picture research: Susie Foster
Project Manager: Ariane Bankes

For the new edition
Managing Editor: Christopher Tinker
Page design: Matthew Young
Production: Ruth Müller-Wirth and Kathleen Bloomfield

Printed and bound in China

Page 2: Detail from Queen Alexandra (1844–1925) by Sir Luke Fildes, 1894 (replica 1920, see page 105). Oil on canvas, 1283 x 1029mm. NPG 1889

Every purchase supports the National Portrait Gallery, London.